AF448521

My Faded Uniform

My Faded Uniform

Dreams, nightmares and waking up again

Stephanie Altus

www.whitefalconpublishing.com

My Faded Uniform
Stephanie Altus

www.whitefalconpublishing.com

In collaboration with

Want Solution
www.wantsolution.com

All rights reserved
First Edition, 2018
Copyright © 2018 Stephanie Altus
Cover design © 2018 by White Falcon Publishing
Cover image © to Stephanie Altus

The author asserts the moral right to be identified as the author of this work.

No part of this publication may be reproduced, distributed, or transmitted in any form or by any means, including photocopying, recording, or other electronic or mechanical methods, without the prior written permission of the author, except in the case of brief quotations embodied in critical reviews and certain other non-commercial uses permitted by copyright law.

Requests for permission should be addressed to
stephanie.altus1@gmail.com

ISBN - 978-93-87193-68-0

Disclaimer

The material in this publication is of the nature of general comment only, and does not represent professional advice. It is not intended to provide specific guidance for particular circumstances and it should not be relied on as the basis for any decision to take action or not take action on any matter which it covers. Readers should obtain professional advice where appropriate, before making any such decision. To the maximum extent permitted by law, the author and publisher disclaim all responsibility and liability to any person, arising directly or indirectly from any person taking or not taking action based on the information in this publication.

Dedication

For Crissy, Jessica and Emily. You girls are my greatest achievement in life, my most steadfast rocks of support, and my biggest inspiration to live with "Joie de vivre" I love you all to the moon and back and more than that.

Foreword

The book you hold in your hands is the remarkable story of a woman we've come to know deeply, and love greatly.

As Steph's Lifestyle and Business Coaches we've had the honour of being by her side as she walked the bumpy road toward her 1 Big Goal. Steph is living proof that courage and commitment can take anyone from where they are to where they want to be.

Steph's journey began with her own Big Goals; like walking the Camino, and writing this book, but her ultimate goal has always been about helping others out of the darkness by shining a light on their 1 Big Goal. As you turn the pages of My Faded Uniform one question we know Steph would love you to ask yourself is; "If I could achieve anything what would it be?" May this book, and Steph's journey inspire you to embrace opportunities and take your own imperfect action toward making the seemingly impossible possible!

Here's to achieving goals & living life by design... not by default

Jodie & Amy
Co-founders of The 7 Effect

It is such an honour for me to be writing this foreword for Steph's book because, over the period of the last one year, our relationship has evolved into one where we take massive risks and explore new worlds together - and that's what this book is a symbol of.

Steph Altus, the author of this book is a woman of great resilience.

She has undergone massive emotional and physical challenges. And no matter what curveball life throws her way, Steph refuses to stop or give up.

She's a woman who personifies country life - free, down-to-earth, sometimes rough, yet always loving, giving and kind.

Everyone has a fall in life. And this book is a story of not only Steph's down time but also how she harnessed the courage that was hiding inside her all along.

She is a woman of great sensitivities and empathy. And this book is her endeavour to help such people who are powerful souls inside, yet for some or the other reason, struggling on the outside, because they have lost their way for a bit.

And through this book, Steph attempts to gently nudge those lost souls to find their path, find their courage and find their voice.

Shilpa Agarwal
Want Solution

Why I Wrote this Book

Have you ever had a dream so big that you were not even sure it was possible to achieve? Have you ever worked so hard and committed your life to make it happen? And have you ever had that dream turn into a nightmare? Slowly, as you begin to emerge from the darkness, you no longer know who you are or where your life is going next. You feel lost and stuck in a rut, unable to function in the life you had and unable to fit into a future yet unknown. Then this is the book that is written for you.

This book is for those who are stuck in a rut following a trauma and feel that there is no light at the end of the tunnel. For the ones who felt they were living the dream, only to have it turn into a nightmare. Mostly, this story is for those who have the courage to dare to dream again and realise that beyond the darkness they can find light and colour in life again.

It contains a raw and open account of my personal experience of having Post Traumatic Stress Disorder (PTSD) and how I perceived my own situation to be at the time.

In reading it, you may recognise some of the feelings and emotions I experienced, however not everyone will identify with every part of it, as everyone has their own unique experience. Everyone has their own perception of what they see, hear, do, and experience in life. It is our own interpretation of the combination of events happening for us in any moment that creates our reality.

As you read through the chapters, you will learn a little about the person I am, how I worked hard to get my dream job and how PTSD took me to some of the darkest moments of my life. You will learn of the courage and resilience it took to work through those black colourless days, of not allowing PTSD to define who I am, of taking a chance, embracing changes, and beginning again to live a life of passion despite still living with PTSD.

Post-traumatic stress disorder (PTSD)[*] is a group of stress reactions that can develop after we witness a traumatic event, such as death, serious injury or sexual violence to ourselves or to others. PTSD can happen after we've been through one traumatic event, or after repeated exposure to trauma. Sometimes, PTSD can develop after hearing details about devastating and traumatic events many times, like the experience of some emergency workers. It's important to seek help to manage PTSD. There are effective treatments for PTSD, and you can feel better.

For anyone who works in a career that exposes them to the trauma and pain of others, there is a higher risk that at some time in your worklife, you may find yourself with a feeling of being trapped, with a shadow overhead - essentially a dark space. The dark space can be different for everyone, though it is generally when you can no longer find happiness in what you do each day, feel a lack of purpose and motivation, or you no longer enjoy life as much as you once did.

---

[*] *Source – blackdoginstitute.org.au*

PTSD and burnout were my blackest place. It was a response to a culmination of all the jobs that I couldn't forget, the nightmares that haunted my sleep, the fatigue of shift work, continuously caring for others with no time left for self-care, missed precious times and moments with those I loved, broken relationships and dysfunctional interactions with others, a broken mind and a broken body.

My experience of PTSD was a clash of many traumatic things that occurred in a short space of time without enough breaks to process each one separately. You often hear people say, "bad things come in threes", in my case there were many more than that and each one seemed worse than the next. I became so overwhelmed by one thing happening, then the next and the next, and it created a situation where I had less of an ability to cope with any of it. I started to fall down a rabbit hole of warped reality, with a mix of emotions and feelings that made little sense to me.

The dark space can be described as a feeling of being stuck in an event or series of events that have changed who you are and how you view life. You seem to have no idea how to integrate back to the life you had, and no idea how to move forward. You often feel drained and exhausted with a tiredness that engulfs your entire being. . You have no words to help others understand what you are experiencing. You feel a massive lack of support, and a feeling of being judged by others, especially if you are meant to be the person who normally cares for others. You are not supposed to be the one who requires being cared for...

I have found that the more people I talk to, the less isolated my experience seems. Most people in life have moments when problems or struggles occur and they try to soldier on and get through it in the best way they can. This is especially true when you work in vulnerable situations where you see pain and tragedy time and again, and it is impossible for this to have no effect on you at all.

For anyone who works in a caring profession, and is stuck in the rut of job fatigue or has been in that dark place, this book can help you to see that you are not alone. This book is designed to resonate with the reader and encourage them to put their hand up and say, "This is happening to me". To open up and talk about it and to get support they need to move forward and find their happiness once more. It is my hope that it opens up discussion, brings people together to support each other in their hard times, and creates an opening for people who are stuck in that rut, to identify and create a new goal or dream to work towards.

The book also provides the readers with a few of the steps I used in dealing with my situation and gives them options that may resonate for them to use in their own journey if they wish. I hope they can be inspired by the fact that they don't have to stay in that dark place and sometimes that's all they need—just that one moment of knowing that it can be different. Then, when they're ready to explore it a bit more, they can use some of the tips provided to find a new direction for their own life.

In that space of darkness and challenge, we can choose to learn about ourselves, to open our eyes to new thoughts, and to question and reframe our beliefs and assumptions. We can become aware of who we are now, after having suffered such adversity. We can embrace the opportunity to make changes and choose our own path forward, and by this process we can find our way back and create a future that is extraordinary.

Everything is possible. Whatever you imagine, you can make it happen. It is clutching that moment of courage and looking into your heart's space, to find what ignites your passion again. It is finding what makes you smile through the tears. It is accepting what happened and allowing it to soften and integrate into your memories without the fear and pain. **It is reconnecting with all the vitality of life!**

The chapters of the book are set in such a manner that you can read all of it, or just flick to the chapter that most resonates with where you feel in the moment. It is a step by step walk through my path of having a dream, making it happen, how it turned into darkness and how I found my way back and built a new dream.

Throughout my journey, I have accepted and used professional help when it was required, and had the ongoing support of family, friends, work colleagues and others in moving through the process to recovery. I have sought coaching and mentoring to identify the parts of me that needed healing and growth, and have gone forward on a journey of learning to follow a new direction. I have come to know that PTSD is something that will not ever just disappear, because the memories are still locked in my mind. However, I now have the ability to live with the pain of the things I have seen without it causing further harm and to live a happy and exciting life, making each day the best it can be.

I have been lucky enough to find the resilience to forge my own path forward. The book contains information that may be of assistance to your circumstances, but it is for each one of us to decide which path we choose to follow.

No-one has to be bound forever by the moments that are difficult. Everyone has the choice to create a new ending and turn themselves into the hero of their own story. This book is the one I needed when the days had no light, and all I saw was the impossibility of my situation. It shows that healing can occur, even if the scars remain. It provides hope and possibility when all seems lost.

Contents

WHO I AM

"Find out who you are and be that person. That's what your soul was put on this earth to be."
Ellen Degeneres

Each stage of our life teaches us more about who we are and where we are in relation to the world around us; how to interact with others and within relationships, how we experience events that occur, and how to survive and thrive in our own individual circumstances.

When we take the time to reflect on who we are and the experiences our life has held, we are better able to understand our reactions to events. From a deep knowing of self, we can find acceptance of ourselves, and in turn others. We can challenge our beliefs and thoughts and lead ourselves to a place of self love. This chapter is a brief overview of my life as a whole and how I used this knowledge to find out who I am and to reconnect with the whole, beautiful, quirky, wild child woman I am. It is with this knowledge that I can move towards building a path that I am once again passionate about, and create an extraordinary future.

Looking back on my life it was a childhood of extremes. I grew up in the bush of the Blue Mountains and was a bit of a wild child. Being the second child of five, I always had someone to spend time with, but it was also easy to be overlooked. I was a happy child and I loved the bush and being in nature. I don't ever remember having a fear in this natural environment. Being quite introverted, I didn't make friends easily, so had only a couple of very close friends. I always stood up for the underdog and would often find myself in trouble when I spoke up for what I saw as injustice being delivered on another person.

We went to church and learnt about right and wrong, attended school and learnt more about how we were expected to behave in society. At school I was the good child, the one who tried to please the teacher by not causing trouble, and helping with the classroom chores.

As girls, we were encouraged to become "Brownies" and it was here we learned about the community and serving others through various volunteering opportunities. Many a weekend morning was spent at the local nursing home helping out the staff with the elderly residents. I loved these moments of seeing how the smallest gestures of help could bring a smile to the face of another person. Reading books to a blind lady is one of my dearest memories. Seeing her face light up at her own memories of a life she could no longer see but held deep in her heart and mind, brought joy to me, even as a young child.

An active child, I loved swimming, dancing, playing netball, softball and walks through my beloved bushland. Some of my fondest memories are of having a fit body, being full of energy and always bounding through days filled with activity and adventure. I was a child who was always moving and trying out new activities, never quite mastering any but always loving the chance to enjoy whatever I was doing.

My parents had their own set of problems. My father was predominantly absent, and my mother was often angry and unable to show love. That being said, there were some "happy family" times I remember, mostly at fire brigade parties and Christmas picnics.

Our home was a place that was a mismatch of either very clean and tidy, or an untidy chaotic mess. The meals we ate were either nurturing and nutritious, or a quick snack that we children made ourselves. Having a mother who was emotionally unstable, with a violent and volatile nature, we never knew how she would be when we saw her. Having an absent father meant we had no shelter or protection from her outbursts. It was a life that was either good or bad; a life of freedom but also fear. We never quite knew which situation we were going to experience at any given moment.

When you grow up with the complete opposites of freedom and fear, you learn to become very resilient. You learn to look after yourself and be self-sufficient. At an early age your life skills become adept and you know how to survive. In the face of fear and anger you learn about coping mechanisms that keep you safe and free from the violence that comes with that level of anger. I became the hidden child at home, the quiet, good girl who tried not to be noticed. In the freedom of the nature and being active, I found curiosity, energy, exuberance and the joy to explore the very essence of life.

As I got older, things became worse at home, so as a very young teenager all I wanted was to get out. For as long as I can remember, I wanted to be a mother and to have a child of my own to love and nurture. My childhood dolls had been my greatest companions when I built cubby houses or played by those mountain streams. I dreamed of a life where I could create a happy and loving family and share that love of nature with them.

My first daughter was born when I was not quite 17 years old. I had all the normal fears about how my mum and others would react to the news, where I would live, how I would afford to raise this child, and would I be able to create this family I had so longed for. Yet, in all of this doubt, I knew that no matter how difficult things were, I would always love my children unconditionally. As a teen mother I would listen to others, but had the confidence to parent my child in my own way, and this continued after the birth of my second child.

With little money, life was simple and I found it was a time that I returned to my roots of freedom and a love of nature. Many days were spent with my baby in the park, at the beach, or walking outside in the fresh air. Moments spent sitting on the grass making daisy chains or exploring the tiny insects that are so abundant in nature. Motherhood brought through my soft side and it was at this time that I felt most connected to my soul and at peace with the role that had been entrusted to me. I loved this part of my life and it still remains my most cherished life moment.

Being a mother was a time that I began to reflect on my experiences of growing up with my own mother. The realisation came to me, of the extent of disconnect that was expressed in my relationship with her. I had so many wonderful memories of fun times with my brothers and sisters, holidays, freedom and family moments. In each of these memories there were only the children together or extended family. My parents were not present in these happy times, Mum was often in the house/cabin alone and Dad had long since left by then. We children were free to wander and amuse ourselves and clearly understood that we were to disturb my mother as little as possible. Throughout my growing years, there were many moves in location and a need to make new friends and start life anew again and again. Thus stability and routine were not a big part of the lessons I learned in life.

As an adult and a mother, I could see my own parents' infallibilities as them doing their best with what they knew from their own life experiences. As a result of having parents who showed little love and affection and were predominantly absent, I now understood where my strong need to be available to my children had come from and why I struggled with parts of my own life.

I could identify the things I had done that felt like failures and know more clearly the people I had hurt or left behind on my own journey. When my marriage crumbled, a deeper understanding of the pain of choices became evident and I struggled with the impact this event had on myself, my girls and others around me. The fight to get back up and keep moving forward became a reality and I was determined to do it in a way that empowered me and my children to make better choices for our future.

As I moved on from the marriage breakdown, I began to expand my world a little more. Many times when I went back and sought support of my parents, I was faced with negativity and condemnation. I remember a particular conversation that sticks in my mind... it was with my dad, just after I had decided to get married for the second time. I rang to ask my dad for some advice about getting a job and what I should do to best earn an income to support my girls and my family. His answer still saddens me to this day. He replied to me that because I had been a high school drop-out and already failed at one marriage, I would have very little likelihood of achieving anything decent in my life or career, and I would achieve nothing with the rest of my life. Wow! What a knock down, but this comment provoked my determination and the resilience that was so much a part of who I was.

Not long before this discussion with my father, I had watched the movie "Legally Blonde" in which a young woman who is portrayed as a ditzy, dumb blonde uses her improbable life experiences as the basis for succeeding in gaining a law degree. This movie became my inspiration to continue my education and I ended up studying and getting my own degree.

In the moment after that conversation, I decided to prove him wrong. I would take my life choices up till then and turn them around to create a success that would show him, myself, my daughters and others what was possible when you believed in a dream.

The cap and gown moment when I received my degree, was shared with my gorgeous daughters and was one of the most poignant and beautiful memories I have. I had taught my daughters that they never had to be defined by another person's opinion of them. It was what was in their hearts and minds that mattered above anything else.

Despite having parents who provided little stability in my life, I was lucky enough to have an amazing Grandpa whose love and support was unconditional. He always showed unwavering belief in me, which instilled a strong sense of being able to attain anything I set my mind on, so long as I believed strongly enough that I could achieve it. My Grandpa nurtured my seemingly crazy dreams by never doubting my ability to make them a reality. He was excited for me when I took on any new challenge, laughed with me, and celebrated my successes. He also helped me get back up after any failures, and supported me to learn and grow from them. He was my constant and taught me to be my own hero.

In these reflections I could see the person I saw myself as - a wild hippy child who craved and loved freedom, variety and adventure. There was a strong determination and resilience in my nature, a deep caring and a strong value of justice and fairness. Connection with others was a difficult concept for me, but once it was there, I had fierce loyalty and sincerity in my relationships. Throughout my life, I have always been an optimistic person, filled with hope; and a bit of a dreamer. Nature, colour, music, and seeing the beautiful in life are the strong themes that are constants in my world.

Life has so many facets and the trick to survival is to look at the whole. If you set a box on a table and then you sit down and look at the box from one side, it just looks like a flat surface. **Then,** if you get up and look at it from a different angle, it becomes a three-dimensional object. When you begin to move around and explore it from all angles, it becomes so much more than a mere box. You can open it, and what it is filled with is determined by what has been placed inside. People are like that box, on the surface we only see one dimension, presented to the world in our first glimpse ofthem. . As we take time to explore and listen, we become aware that there is so much more and each person is like a Pandora's box, filled with an array of experiences.

Embrace all of you, the decisions and experiences that create joy, as well as those that cause angst or sorrow. Spending some time in self-reflection can lead to growth and self-acceptance. Once you come to accept who you are in all your aspects and facets, it is here you will find self-love. You can begin to define a life path that fills your soul and brings happiness to your world.

There is no such thing as failure, there is only learning. When you are able to grow and make another choice from something that did not go as per plan, it is here that you stretch your own boundaries and beliefs and become a bigger and better version of you.

If you are unable to believe in yourself, find someone who does believe in you. Surround yourself with the people you aspire to be, those whom you admire and who are already achieving the results and life you are seeking. Learn from them and follow in their footsteps to become all the potential you see in yourself.

Through all of this, maintain a sense of self and hold on to your own individuality. Add a little spice of who you are to all you do. You are the best person to be you!

What was your childhood like growing up? How has your life been influenced by your life as a child? What are the things that you love about yourself and that make you your unique self?

Learnings from this chapter…

To answer these questions and become your most authentic self:

1. Take time to reflect back and remember who you were as a child. Think about the things you loved, and the courage and tenacity you had that brought you right to this moment now.
2. Embrace all of you. If it were not for what you have already experienced you would not be this person you are today.
3. Use that self acceptance as the foundation to build the next version of who you choose to become and add a little of the spice of who you are to everything you do.
4. There is no failure, only growth and learning from the things that don't work out.

VISIONS IN TRAGEDY

"Life has an infinite number of moments and any of these can change your life in an instant."
Stephanie Altus

There are moments that have the ability to change the course of your life. It may be something that happens and opens up just a second of possibility for what may be. It may prompt a memory that brings joy or pain to your present. It may be a feeling that all is as it should be for you in that time, and you are exactly where you want to be. It may be a strong intuition that you need to change direction and do something different with your life. This chapter is about some of those moments in my own life and how each one has changed the direction of my life.

When these moments occur it is a choice point. We get to choose if, when and how we react to the situation at hand. Perhaps we may take action immediately, or sometimes we just notice the moment, add it to our memory and keep going with life as it is, because the time is just not right for us. Either way, the things you notice become a part of your thoughts and have the potential to alter your life path.

One of these moments came for me so many years ago. After a family tragedy, I was called to the place where it had occurred. I arrived to a scene of police cars and an ambulance taking up most of the street. As I rushed into the house, I was met by overwhelming pain, disbelief and uncertainty. Glancing across the room, I noticed a female paramedic standing quietly by the kitchen. She offered to make me a cup of tea and as she handed me the cup I saw the tears in her eyes that held all the sadness of empathy.

In that second I knew that being a paramedic was something that I wanted to do. To help and support someone in their worst moment with genuine care seemed like a rewarding career to aspire to. In the darkness of death I saw a glimmer of possibility for what may be. At that specific point in time I was a busy mother with a new baby and a school aged child, andin dealing with this tragic time, I didn't have the capacity for this idea to be more than a fleeting thought. Never the less, a seed had been planted.

Through the darkness of unexpected death I spent a long time working through the grief, and it seemed that I had so many questions with no answers. There were all the what-ifs, all the maybes, and all the whys? When things are bad we all ask these questions and search for a meaning to make sense of it. I searched many places for information, and sought support from others who might have some inkling of understanding. I delved into how the body works, religion, philosophy, self-awareness and a multitude of other information to try and find some meaning to what had happened. Over the months and years, I learned a lot more about myself and about life. I finally found acceptance that sometimes there are no answers to the questions we ask.

Instead I learnt to change the questions. I began to ask HOW? How can I use this awful event to help others, how can I live my life better as a result of this experience? How can I find meaning and become a better person from what this has taught me? And I realised that by changing the question I was no longer stuck in the pain, I had moved forward to a space of possibility.

As I read information to gain more understanding of that tragedy, it was always with the thought of seeking a purpose to use the knowledge for some good. I began to notice what was needed to support others who were going through this same situation. I took action to create things I could do to help others, which helped me to engage in life again, and the sadness of missing our family member became integrated into who I had become.

This death had not created drastic changes in my life, rather subtle ones that made me more compassionate and empathetic. It made me cherish my time with my loved ones more deeply and it opened up my mind to where I had gained an understanding that the world is not based on my beliefs alone. My conscious awareness of the different ideas and perceptions of how others experienced life had expanded. I learned to be empathic and understanding when people's beliefs did not match my own and to respect each individual's opinions.

The years passed and I found myself in a different space and time of my life, in quite a different set up, when another series of events occurred. By now we were living on a farm which was at quite a distance from the town. This was a time just before my marriage broke up and my life felt like it was in tatters. I was a stay-at-home mum whose children were now both at school, and I was looking for something that inspired me to fill the empty moments while my kiddies were away all day.

Many moments on the farm opened my eyes to the potential for injury and I began to think about how far away from help we were. One night at home the girls broke a mirror and as I went to survey the damage, I noticed that my youngest child had cut her hand. Cleaning her up, it was a very tiny cut and a band-aid would suffice this time. I wondered what I would have done if the cut had been worse. Soon after, on a weekend at home, my girls were playing on the trampoline and one bounced too close to the edge and fell off and hit her head on the gravel path. Although she wasn't badly hurt, this was the moment I became aware that I did not know what to do if she had been more seriously injured. I remember thinking in this instant that an ambulance would have to come from some 30 or more minutes away and this could be the difference between life and death if something significant had happened.

The next morning after taking the girls to school, I stopped to buy the local paper and read it at the coffee shop before heading home. There was nothing exciting about this, as it was something I did every week. On this particular day however, I noticed an advertisement saying that the nearest ambulance station was seeking people who were interested in becoming volunteer ambulance officers. In taking up the offer, you would receive free first aid training. My mind returned to that death all those years ago, and memories of the paramedic who had been so kind on such a horrible day. I knew that the time was now right for me to make a change in my life. The seed that had been planted at a time long past, had now begun to set down roots and was ready to grow. This monment in life was a choice point. Later that morning, I found the courage to ring the number to get the information about the course, and a new journey began.

It was not to be so easy though! My rocky marriage had ended that week and I didn't yet know how to be alone bringing up my children. I had no job or income and no skills I could identify, that would help me to find work. I had a very tiny network of support and if I wanted to attend this first aid training I would have to find someone to look after my girls on the training nights. I wasn't used to being around other people, especially ones I didn't know. My self-confidence was at an all-time low, and I had no idea if I could even do the course because I had been a high school drop-out. This was another dark moment in my life, and I felt like a complete failure.

We all have these grey moments in our lives. Things that bring us sadness, confusion, anger, grief and all the emotions that don't make us feel good. In these times we need to allow ourselves to feel the emotion and give ourselves enough space and time to integrate the event into that which we have become because of the experience.

Begin with being kind to yourself, care for yourself in the way you would treat a friend going through the same situation. Seek support and accept offers of help, balance it with alone time to reflect. Nurture your body with simple, good, healthy food. Spend some time doing light, easy exercise, and have a little time outdoors each day. Be gentle on yourself and do things only as you feel ready. Find small things to do each day that bring a sense of achievement. Don't rush the process, it will happen in its own time and way, and one day you will look back and find that you have moved forward. You are now in a completely new phase of your life.

This time for me was now. The roots had taken hold and were stronger than my fear. I was about to enter a whole new chapter of my life.

Do you have a moment in your life that caused you great difficulty or pain? What did that experience teach you? How did you move forward to be at this point in your life?

Learnings from this chapter…

If you can identify with any of the views expressed in this chapter, remember:

1. We all have moments of sadness and difficulty in our lives. Understand that this is normal and you will learn to move forward again.
2. There are questions in life that cannot be answered. Accept this and begin to ask different questions.
3. Everyone experiences their own journey after a tragedy. Take the time and self care you need to overcome the difficult moments in life.
4. Our beliefs are how we perceive the world around us and each person has their own individual perception of this. Beliefs are not set in concrete and as we experience more growth and learning in life, our own beliefs can be changed, expanded or deleted as we choose.

A NEW PATH

*"From a tiny acorn seed grows the great and
mighty oak tree."*
Thomas Fuller

Have you ever had a time in your life where everything seems broken and the reality of life is nothing like the dreams you started out with? And when it has all crumbled, you are left with no choice but to pick up the pieces and design a new creation.

The day I read that newspaper advertisement for volunteer ambulance officers, I knew this was a new path I wanted to take, but I had no idea how I was going to make it happen.

My perfectly planned happy family was no longer a reality and with few skills, uncompleted schooling, and poor self esteem, this idea to become an ambulance officer seemed well above the realm of what I could achieve. As an overweight, unfit mother and housewife who was socially isolated, living on a farm at 30 minutes' drive from the local town, and now single with no income. The dream seemed impossible! Having a great intolerance to the smell of blood made me doubt my ability even further and I had huge fear about being in a class with people, when I didn't yet know anyone.

Greater than my fear, was the deep desire that had been planted as a seed on the night of the family tragedy, and doing this course was a practical choice to have knowledge of first aid to provide help if it was ever needed. I strongly believed the time was right and the universe had delivered this moment to me. Now I just needed to be brave enough to take the first step and follow the journey ahead.

Here I was in a whole new phase of my life and starting over. In my heart it felt right but in my mind there was so much doubt and negative self-talk. My children were both at school and I had the time to study, but walking into an unfamiliar situation alone was not something I had ever done. People like me didn't do things like this. My safe space was being a mother and providing for my children, not out there in the big wide world of the unknown.

I remember sitting outside in my car before I went into that first meeting. My head filled with self-judgement about what these people would think of me. As I sat there, I remembered that little girl who had loved adventure and had no fear of being out there in the bush. I breathed in that courage, got out of the car and stepped inside. I didn't know, in that moment, that this was to become the start of the biggest and most exciting path I had ever taken up till now in my life. It was also a path that would take me to the very lowest point in my life more than once, and then back again and in a whole other new direction.

After that initial training night, I felt a hint of excitement rise inside me. It ignited a fire that lit up the potential I could see, of the huge changes this could bring to my life. Now I was ready to take on the challenge and if I could create the vision and focus strongly enough, then maybe I could work my way up to become a paramedic.

Once I started, I found that I actually loved it, even though I knew nothing about working in the medical field. Learning about the body and how it works became my new passion and I embraced all the knowledge that was still so foreign to me. Soon, I progressed from first aid to working as an ambulance officer and my world took on a totally new facet.

Volunteering increased my confidence, forced me to engage with people and each shift left me with a sense of satisfaction for the service I was providing to my local community. I loved helping people and knowing I was making a difference.

My children were thriving, and we were all growing and learning new things each day. We expanded our awareness as we mingled with the society a little more deeply, but still loved our quiet time as we sat together doing our homework each night. Each job stretched my knowledge and my boundaries and with every patient I attended my beliefs and values were moulded into a broader perspective.

For each step of action I took towards embracing this new path, I was rewarded with opportunities that I had never known before. Alongside the ambulance officer training, I started to do short courses at a local community centre, which led me to enroll in TAFE to complete my education. The world now felt like a bigger and brighter place. I remember one of my favourite moments was when I got the chance to spend a few days working with the air ambulance. Going in a plane seemed like an inconceivable dream, but now I had done it. I loved flying and this opened up an even bigger sphere of possibility for my future. The greatest benefit that came was building a network of support around me and making connections, some of which would go on to become lifetime friendships.

This was a scary but fun time in my life. Being a mum was still my number one passion but at the same time I had a growing desire to explore this new dimension in more detail. Being a paramedic had now become my non–negotiable goal.

Most of all, I knew that I had been willing to take a risk. I could have shrunk back into the darkness of divorce and failure, but instead I was willing to say yes. Even though I didn't know how I would manage it, I knew I would work it out as I went along. I had embraced the fear and still had the courage to take on each new stride. I had taken back my power to define myself and forge my own trail forward.

I ask you, do you have that inkling of a spark inside you? Are you stuck at a choice point and not sure which tangent is best for you right now?

Learnings from this chapter...

If this is you, here are my hot tips for taking that next teetering step –

1. If there is something that you notice around you that makes you go "WOW" - be prepared to take a risk and give it a go.
2. If you are not sure whether you can do something, say yes anyway, then work out the how as you go along. We are much more competent than we think we are, and the expert first has to be a novice and learn.
3. Once you take action , momentum happens and you find it becomes easier as you consistently work towards your goal. Embrace all the opportunities and don't be afraid to dream big.

———— CHAPTER 4 ————

LEARNING AND GROWTH

*"Life is a meandering path towards unknown destinations.
the joy is in the journey."*
Stephanie Altus

Do you remember a time when you decided to do something new? What it felt like when you started in uncertainty as a novice? As you grow and learn, the fear diminishes and you become comfortable in the journey towards expertise.

This chapter tells about the journey of working as an unpaid volunteer, through the different roles I undertook, until I felt ready to apply for a job as a paramedic. It includes the successes and the trials and tribulations that come in times of massive learning, change, and growth.

In the last chapter I spoke about my love of the job, and how I had now come to realise that this was exactly what I wanted to do. I knew I had the surety, focus and commitment to keep going until I attained the final goal of becoming a paid paramedic. Along the way to achieving this One Big Goal, there were many side paths and convolutions in the journey. There were times I wandered from the road I was travelling. There were phases of stopping in one place for a while to allow for the adjustments in my life and my family. It was here that I found the biggest growth and learnt to be myself, while adjusting my style to the ever changing situations that I was faced with.

The world tells us, through media and opinion, how we should feel, how we should live, how life should be, what timelines we need to be following. Often, what we're being told is not congruent with how we are feeling. We start to believe we are doing things wrong or being judged on our actions. We can begin to shut down and stop living life in the way that makes us happy.

The first harsh lesson I learnt was that society is full of stereotyping. I had been a middleclass wife, with two beautiful children, living in a nice town. Now, here I was - a divorced, single mother who had no job or income, uncompleted education, no money and not much idea what my future held. My perception of the stereotype I was being labeled with was one of bludging off the welfare system, sitting at home all day, drinking coffee and having a lazy life supported by the working population. My belief at that time was deeply ingrained and I thought that to be respected, I would have to work hard and get a job to support myself and my kids. I was my own worst judge and jury. Although I didn't know it at the time, this was to be my greatest downfall in the years ahead.

Any job that provides a service to people requires the worker to learn about others, and how they respond in certain situations. This is especially vital to understand in the stressful situations that are naturally encountered in emergency service work. I had to get to know myself and how I responded to the chaos and crisis that often confronted me on jobs. Remember, one of the things that I really didn't tolerate was the smell of blood. I didn't hate the thought or sight of it, and it didn't scare me, but I had to teach myself to endure the smell of it. This was easy in the adrenaline rush of an emergency work because my mind was so focused on the patient and the steps I needed to take to treat them. I learnt from this, that we can change our perceptions of what we can and cannot do.

The education component was a style that worked well for me because much of it was hands-on and self-paced study at home. Despite this there was a huge amount of theory and I had been a high school drop-out. I didn't yet think I would know how to study or effectively take in all this information and remember it. So, I devised a system that worked for me. Our intake class created a study group and practiced the skills by doing regular scenarios. As we worked through each potential job situation, we incorporated the theory for what we were practicing. As I passed each exam, my confidence grew and I began to drop the belief that I was dumb and uneducated.

Our beliefs about ourselves come from all our experiences and relationships in our lives. If we are taught at a young age to behave in a certain ways, what is acceptable and what is not and how life should be lived, we grow up surmising that how we live is how it should be. As we get older and experience more of life, these beliefs get challenged and stretched. We start to think in a more open way, and wonder all that we have known till now is true, and decide if what we choose to believe still fits for where we are in our life currently.

My vision of becoming a paramedic was growing increasinglyvivid. Each day I could see more and more clearly that this role provided the challenge, autonomy and satisfaction that I craved. I now believed that I had the ability to do anything I set my mind to do.

Being an ambulance officer exposed me to a world I had never known before. Suddenly I was interacting with people who lived life in very different ways to mine. Their relationships were different to mine, their living spaces were different to what I had ever seen, they spoke in a language that I didn't yet understand even though it was still English, they understood life in different ways. It was at this time I learnt that my way of being and living was a very narrow map of the world. To move forward in this career I had chosen, I would need to approach it with a very open mind, and be ready to leave my beliefs, opinions and perspectives at home, if I was to be able to give the best of myself in this role.

This realisation allowed me to tap into another part of me that is what I call intuition or gut feeling. It is when we follow what our gut and our heart tells us to do. Every step of the way through my life, this has been a part of me. When something feels absolutely right I will do it, even if I cannot see all the steps of how it may work. It has always been a good guide for me in my life. More and more I began to rely on my intuition to know what stance I needed to take for the best communication and outcome for each patient. Along with the knowledge and skills I was acquiring, I found myself easily adjusting my own style to that needed by every patient I encountered. To this day I am not entirely sure if intuition is innate in us, or comes from a place of exposure and previous experience. Perhaps it is a combination of both and I have learned to trust my own truth of this. .

The steepest learning curve for me in this journey was to define my boundaries. As a naturally caring person, I would always go above and beyond to help others. At times this came at the expense of my own wellbeing and life balance. I would find myself saying yes to extra shifts when it was hard to get a crew. This would break into my family time and leave me in a state of conflict about my role as a mother. Colleagues would ask for help and I would say yes and go and help them. Sometimes this was at the expense of my own study or time with my friends.

Many jobs tugged at my heart strings and I wanted to provide more for the patient than the job required. Each time I encountered a patient with a sad story beyond their illness or injury, I wanted to help fix their problems. I remember an older lady who was reluctant to go to hospital because she had no family or friends to feed her cat, but she was very unwell and needed to go. My heart space wanted to offer to feed the cat for her while she was away, but this fell far outside the parameters of the job I was doing. If I provided this extra service to every patient that needed help, I would have had little time left for what was most important in my own life.

Working in a small regional town also held its challenges. Neighbours, patients and other members of the community would see me in the shops on my days off, and would approach me and want to talk to me about a particular job or situation. Whilst this was usually from a genuine place of concern, care and interest, these were conversations that were often of a confidential nature, and I was unable to engage in them. Finding a conversation that was polite, tactful and respectful, but didn't include information that I was not able to discuss, was a skill I quickly learnt. One served me well at that time, and I found it transposed to other areas of my life. There were other boundaries I had to define along the way, and I had to decide what was acceptable to me, to my job role I, and to expectations of the community I was serving, and to others who may be affected by my words or actions.

Moving from being a wife and stay-at-home mum was one of the biggest transformations I have experienced in my life to date. From being a quiet stay-at-home person who was often afraid to step out and speak up for myself I now found myself as a confident and community-minded woman who believed in her own power. I was working to achieve a massive goal and I was having fun and enjoying the journey. I had stretched my personal and professional boundaries in an incredibly vast way. I had stepped outside the walls of my own comfort zone and allowed the expansion by saying yes to more and more new experiences. I had worked out those boundaries of mine that I was unprepared to break or breech, which allowed me to live in congruence with what mattered most to me. And I learned which ones I was prepared to stretch, to allow me to chase my dreams and pursue a life that was so much more exciting and extraordinary.

Throughout this time, the one thing that helped me to get over the hurdles and manage the difficult moments was to surround myself with people who supported and believed in me. I sought out people I admired who were already where I wanted to be and doing what I aspired to do. I gathered with those who believed in me and even when I faltered, they would keep the dream alive for me. I celebrated with those who truly understood the energy and effort that was expended to take each step. I chose a mentor who offered advice and gave me the next step when I became unsure. Most especially, I went back to my Grandpa. I talked with him and shared all the joy and fear that was inside my mind and heart. Never once did he doubt that I was going to reach my goal. His excitement and happiness for me was a tangible feeling which he fed into my heart, to hold and cherish whenever I needed an extra boost.

Like the caterpillar that transforms into a butterfly, there was an emerging from a cocoon of self-doubt into a world of possibility. This is a time of change and an evolution of becoming more of who we can be. Through the struggle that comes from the unfolding of our new wings, we flourish into the best version of ourselves. Like the butterfly, we need the wrestling and grappling to strengthen and reinforce our resilience. Immense patience and persistence are required if we are to truly become strong enough to survive in this new world we are now a part of.

The world now held a huge new perception for me, one of possibilities and choices. It was okay to say yes to options and it was also okay to say no to what didn't fit into my life anymore.

Each one of us is unique, and we all come from our own experiences. Even those brought up in the same household can have different perception and different memories of what mattered most to them. If we go back to the box analogy, each person sees the box from where they are currently standing. If we dare to take a risk and move and explore, we begin to see more facets of the box and build a bigger and more complete picture of what it actually is or could be. When we add imagination, creativity and potential, the simple box becomes a whole realm of creations that it may become.

People are like the box, we can all evolve and become so much more than what we believe in or know if we are able to open our minds and hearts, set about attempting new things, and say yes to choices that come our way. Bring that vision of what could be to life, add colour and pizzaz to it, make it larger and brighter, add things of value and discard the unwanted, and begin working towards making dreams into reality.

Through this growth and learning I got from being a volunteer, the world opened up to become a bit larger. I began the journey down the path towards getting the job I now longed for. The job that had been planted as a seed so many years before.....

Learnings from this chapter...

Dare to take a risk and don't be afraid to give new things a go. You never know where one leap of faith may lead you.

1. Know yourself! Learn who you are and what your values and beliefs are. What has influenced and guided you up till now and created these ideas? Do these thoughts still serve you well in the space your life is at this point in time?
2. Know your boundaries. What are your non-negotiable goals that keep you safe and living the life you want? Which ones can be stretched and expanded to create an even bigger and more dynamic life experience?
3. When you cannot believe in yourself, find someone who believes in you. Allow them to champion and support you until you are left with no doubt that you can achieve your goals.
4. Life is a constant flux of learning and growth, embrace it! You may just find you are not the boxed version of yourself that you are in this moment. Use all of your imagination and creativity to create more possibility and a clearer vision of the dream you are working towards.

TOWARDS THE GOAL

"You Get by achieving your goals is not as important as what you become by achieving your goals."
Henry David Thoreau

Any goal or dream that matters enough will create equal amounts of exhilaration and fear. Reaching a goal takes a clear focus on what you want and how to get there, a big enough reason to keep taking action towards it, determination to work hard, patience, resilience, optimism and passion. So many people know what they would like in life but never take that first step to start towards it, or they give up as soon as the going gets tough.

Working as a volunteer in a role I was passionate about, gave me lots of insight into what attitude and skills would be required to succeed in gaining a paid position as a paramedic. Working hard and building a good reputation were only a small part of the traits needed to be proficient in the role. Also required were the ability to remain calm despite chaos, ongoing training and learning new skills and knowledge, critical thinking, being able to communicate and connect with people across a broad complexity of personalities, resilience and a sense of fun. And this was just the tip of the iceberg!

Over time I built respect from my colleagues and was always a willing student, ready to ask and take on any new aspects of the job that I didn't yet know. I forged positive working relationship that supported and nurtured the path I was on. My role as a mother remained my most valued position but I was now setting new and stronger roots ready to emerge as a strong sapling in the world of all things ambulance. This goal had other ideas for me though, and in no way was mine going to be a linear journey to becoming a paramedic.

Have you ever decided to take a road trip to a predetermined destination? Sometimes it is easy and you drive straight to your destination, arriving without any delay. Other times there are detours, delays and distractions that take you off route and through other places that were never part of the plan. Take a journey with me through this chapter and discover that success is sometimes more than a straight highway to your arrival.

After two years into my volunteer role I put in my first application to be a paramedic, attended the interview and waited. Rejection! Then I put in a second application. Rejection again!

This second rejection became another choice point in my life. I could give up, I could choose to believe I was not good enough to be a paramedic, or I could learn what else I needed to do that would give me a better chance when applying again. I could opt to take a detour that would improve my chances of success in my next interview or I could change focus and take an entirely new direction.

I chose to take a detour and continue my journey to becoming a paramedic, albeit along a different road. I asked questions about where my interview had not gone so well and I sought out other jobs that related to the paramedic role to increase my experience and exposure to the work. I became an enrolled nurse to start to learn more about patient care and having a profession in the medical field.

Even though this was not exactly what the dream was, I pursued it with passion and gave 100% to being the best nurse I could be. I enjoyed the work but never lost sight of the bigger dream. Over time, a job came up as a paid Non Emergency Ambulance Officer and this felt like one step closer to my ideal destination. This time when I attended the interview I ended up being successful in getting the job. As this job was casual, I maintained my nursing whilst becoming the best ambulance officer I could.

I thrived in the job as an ambulance officer. I loved working in a position that allowed me to care for and help people with the freedom of not being stuck working inside a building every day. I loved the variety of every job being different and the camaraderie of the people I worked with. It never bothered me that this was the non-emergency side of the work, instead my focus was on continuing to learn and grow and build an even more respected reputation.

Some years into this job I secured a position in a newer hybrid ambulance role. This was a mixture of non-emergency and emergency work in which, as an ambulance officer, I worked with a paramedic. Wow, now I felt I had moved one step closer to the bigger dream. I relished the excitement and exhilaration of the emergency side of the work, while still loving the calm of the transport side of this job. It felt like the best of both worlds and I could now leave behind my nursing and focus on my ambulance career.

The ongoing education from this role was a constant but gentle slope to climb, and the balance of being a mother and my work life began to gain equilibrium. While I still aspired to the role of a paramedic, I was content and happy in the job I was doing and in life. This was a time that was filled with many opportunities that became the shiny distractions to working towards my ultimate dream.

As life cruised along and I became more proficient at my job, my children were growing up rapidly. I started to feel that gnawing passion to achieve my ultimate goal to be a paramedic growing again. As I watched and worked with the paramedics, I admired the extra skills and knowledge they had, and the extra care and help they could give a patient in emergency situations. My thirst for new learning and knowledge grew and I felt a restlessness to start moving forward again. An advertisement came up for student paramedics and once again I applied. Rejection! Oh no, how did that happen?

This was yet another choice point in life and again, I could choose my destiny. After finding out what didn't go well in this interview process, I made up my mind to get back on track and work harder towards my dream of being a paramedic. This time I was ready to do whatever it took and not stop until I had achieved this ultimate goal. My first step was to choose a mentor to guide me towards being the person I needed to be and I listened, really listened, and learnt so much from her. I imitated her attitude, behaviour, professionalism, and her language until they became a part of my own persona.

I gleaned from my interview debrief that the study required as a student paramedic was intense. It would require loads of self-discipline and focus to pass the exams to become a fully qualified paramedic. Up until that time I had little education experience at the level that was deemed to be necessary for success.

It was at this time that I remembered the movie I had watched a few years prior. The movie was "Legally Blonde" and in that instant I was inspired to set a new goal on the path to my bigger destination. I knew the time was right to apply to undertake getting a degree at university. If Elle Woods could succeed in getting a degree, despite being seen as a dumb blonde, then I had every chance of also being able to achieve it. Taking the step into the world of university education was a whole new mountain to conquer, but I was determined to use this to teach my girls that anyone can follow a dream and make it happen. Even a high school drop-out could succeed in the education realm.

The journey was speeding up now and taking me through places I had never dreamed existed. I loved this new ride and consistently worked hard to get through each topic, ticking them off one at a time. All the while, I ensured I was giving 100% to my job and becoming a better version of the person that would succeed in being a paramedic.

Two years into my degree, and with loads of mentoring and much more growth and knowledge, I again applied for a position as a paramedic. Success! My dream was not yet achieved though - I now had two years ahead of me as a student paramedic before I would qualify and

I could truly say I had arrived at that destination I had set myself so many years before. My very fondest memory is of visiting my Grandpa to tell him the news, and the joy and excitement we shared in that time together. Sadly, this was to be the last time I saw him.

The road of being a student paramedic was one of mountains and valleys. Long climbs upwards, to be rewarded with beautiful views, gentle cruising along the straight plains of time between assessments, sometimes conquering rough patches on the road. At other times, stopping to meet up with friends and celebrate each phase of the course we passed. As a student paramedic, I loved the challenge, and found it thrilling rather than scary or difficult.

To ensure success in our studies and to become the best paramedics we could be, we joined forces as a student group and supported each other through our study. The knowledge and skills I needed at this level were far greater than I had ever experienced and I wondered how I would ever learn and remember it all. I teamed up with a friend who had also got into the job at the same time, and together we sought mentors to help us practice and quiz us on our understanding of what we were learning.

My home became a shrine to the study I was undertaking and my daughters inadvertently learnt right along with me due to the constant exposure to my notes and practice sessions. Imagine this – my lounge room and toilet walls papered in A4 sheets of diagrams, flow charts and dot point notes. Even my friends thought I had gone a little crazy.

It was in this time I got the first inkling of the potential for recurring memories that brought hopelessness to my mind. During our trauma study block we were asked what job we thought would be the absolute worst imaginable job we might attend. My answer was a significant burns job.

Later in the week of that same trauma block, we were shown a video of a train accident. As I watched, the tears pricked at my eyes and a clear and vivid memory of being at that place in that moment flashed into my mind. As a child I had been at the scene of that particular train crash, and the memory had been buried deep in my mind until now. I easily composed myself and continued to focus on my study.

On my first rotation of shifts on the road after the trauma study block in the college, my worst thought became reality as we were dispatched to a serious burns case. Have you ever had a time where you feared something and then your worst fear was happening right in front of you? Reflecting after the case, I realised that I had done the job without faltering. The automaticity of what I had learned till now had served me well and I had been able to complete the job with focus and curiosity. A false sense of security set in after this night and I now held the belief that whatever was presented to me within the job, I would be able to handle.

It was not long after, I completed my course and was now a fully qualified paramedic. I had done it! I had achieved the dream and reached my goal. The seed that had been planted some 20 years before had nurtured into a full grown tree.

At our graduation ceremony I remember the happiness I felt as I stood with my fellow classmates and we were handed our diplomas. The vision I had held so long was now my reality. I was a qualified paramedic, being paid to do a job I was passionate about.

Over the two years of my paramedic studies so much had happened in my life and the journey had contained many, many twists and turns. Getting married again, the death of my beloved Grandpa, buying a house, illness and surgery, the sickness of one of my beautiful daughters, and adjusting to the routine being a shift working mother and wife.

During this time, I had deferred my degree studies and now the time was right to go back and complete it. It was a smaller goal but one that still fired a passion in me. I no longer felt the need to do it to prove to myself or my girls, that anyone could get education despite their background. Instead I could focus on finishing it for the pleasure and sense of achievement. It became about the fun of throwing my cap in the air at the graduation ceremony and proudly accepting my rolled up parchment secured with a satin ribbon. Remembering the scene in "Legally Blonde" where Elle attended her graduation was my inspiration to finish my degree.

The day I actually stood on that stage knowing my two daughters were in the audience, there was no fear of being in front of hundreds of people, there was just a feeling of completion and a deep knowing inside me, that anything is possible. For the first time ever in my life I felt worthy and capable. I had achieved this! I realised in that moment the extent of the growth I had experienced from that first hesitant day when I sat in my car outside a first aid course.

Life now seemed like I had reached the destination, and I had time to stop and reflect and enjoy the place I was in. It had not been a fast or easy trek to arrive at my seemingly perfectplace. There were many people and moments that had influenced and supported my journey along the way, and there were many nay-sayers who doubted my ability or actively discouraged me from continuing to follow my dream. However I had stood firm, run the good race and come out victorious.

There was still much to learn and all this new knowledge had to be integrated into doing each and every job. I knew that rather than the end, this was just anotherbeginning.

Learnings from this chapter...

1. When you have a 1 Big Goal, give it your best shot. If it doesn't work out but it is still your passion - don't give up, try it again in a new way. There is no failure, just learning the ways that don't work. Persistence can pay off in the end.

2. You never know what you are capable of until it is done. If you are not sure what you want to do or whether you can achieve it, find someone who can teach you. Find a mentor or get yourself a coach to support and assist you. This is also true when you falter or stall. A mentor or coach can help you to refocus, set smaller steps to follow and get you moving forward again.

3. Goals and dreams require focus, determination, action steps, patience and passion if they are to become reality. No one can do the work for you because it is only you who can make it happen. Having that one special person on your side, that believes in you and celebrates each small success, makes the journey easier.

4. The reward is worth it. Celebrate and share it with those who matter the most.

IT GETS REAL

"Don't trust everything you see. Even salt looks like sugar."
Maryum Ahsam

Have you ever completed a goal and felt the pride and satisfaction of finishing it? What comes next? It may be that the end is just the start, or you may look for a new project. You often reflect on different ways you could have achieved this goal instead and use it to move onto your next goal. Human nature seems to be that once we achieve one big dream, it is not long before we are in the 'what next' phase. We begin to look for our next achievement. What else can we do? What can we add to this to make it better? What other things are out there, or what have we put aside that we can go back to? Life is a never ending journey of movement forward onto the next thing and then the next, and the next.

As a paramedic, every day and every job is different. My passion for the job was like a fire and I continued to acquire experience and knowledge from every case

I attended. I loved the autonomy and freedom the job gave me to make decisions, and provide care for each patient depending on their individual need. I loved the variety and excitement of the emergency nature of the role, and the black humour that helped us to cope with situations that are often too hard to see.

However, the job of a paramedic is tainted with uncertainty and stress. Never really knowing what you will see when you arrive at a job, not always being able to make a positive difference to a patient, long shifts over a 24-hour roster, missing important family moments and not being able to tell others of the horrors you have seen during a shift.

The reality of the job hit me early in my career. I followed the rules and implemented the skills and information I had been taught in my student days, but I soon identified that no patient is a text book case and no job can be narrowed down perfectly to a flow chart.

The college can teach you what to do and the practical aspects of the skills required. They can teach you how to use the equipment and how to ask for help when a job is beyond your scope of practice. Added to the course are pictures of scenes that help expose you to scenarios you may see. There is advice provided on how to care for yourself when you have difficulty coping with a job, and how to recognise stress in yourself and your workmates.

Attending cases is a lot more complex than the simplicity taught in college. I could soon identify that I was an over thinker. I analysed and questioned many aspects of each job, and I wanted to know and understand in greater depth what was happening, why and what else I might have done. I wanted to give every patient the ultimate care that I could possibly provide.

It is a good thing to keep expanding your awareness and ability in your chosen area of expertise. From being a novice, to becoming an expert takes practice and continued and ongoing learning of skills and information in your chosen field. In many careers, it is an ever dynamic process as theories are tested and understanding and awareness expands. Health is an area where many confounding and conflicting situations arise to complicate even the simplest of presentations. Each and every patient is an individual and what works in one situation is not viable in another. So many factors determine what outcome each job will present.

This reminds me of a little ditty I was once told that for me reflects the changing dynamics in perfect words. "Normal is an illusion. What is normal for the spider is chaos for the fly" – by Charles Addams. It means that a web for a spider is normal as part of their being, but this same web is chaos for the fly when it gets caught up in it and inevitably is eaten by the spider. The same can be said for patients in medical emergencies. What is a small cough for one patient, may be a desperate fight for every breath in another. Or what may be a minor injury in one individual may mean a traumatic death in another. When it comes to humans, there are no exact rules. Rather, there are a combination of signs and symptoms, all wrapped up in the patient's own individual responses emotionally and physically, to what is happening to them in that moment. This becomes more perplexing when you factor in the uncontrolled environments that are part of many jobs, and the information that can be provided from the differing perspectives of the patient and others in attendance. Add to this, that each job is walking into a relative unknown, and until you areon the scene, words often do not describe what you are about to encounter.

All these things are the bits that no amount of learning in the classroom can prepare you for. Another aspect that cannot be preempted is each paramedic's individual reaction to how they experience a job, or how another colleague may respond on the same case. For each situation it is a symphony of the unique experiences of each and every individual involved, and no job will ever be a replica of another.

An example of this is when ten people witness any one incident. On questioning about what happened, each of the ten will give a slightly different variation of what actually happened. All the accounts are factual and correct, just given from the perspective of the person telling it. This is because they may have seen it from different angles, the acuity of their various senses may differ, their previous life experiences and beliefs play a role in how they interpret the information. How the incident has impacted them also has an influence and effect on their behaviour at the scene and what information they might provide.

An early experience occurred for me, where a patient died unexpectedly. Due to my naivety in the job and a plethora of other factors, I was not able to grasp or fathom why the job had run the way it had. I found myself questioning each and every action I had taken, the level of my understanding of the knowledge and skills I had learned, how I would do the job differently if I encountered a similar scene, and what trust and safety I had in asking for help for the parts I didn't yet understand. At some point much later I became aware that this job was extra complex and the outcome was exactly as expected, but in that moment in my career, I did not have enough experience to know that.

It was this job that brought to me an awareness of the culture of keeping up a facade of being tough. To keep up the appearance that we could cope with anything we came across in the ever changing scenes we attended. All these years ago, there was an unspoken rule that if you couldn't deal with what you saw out there on jobs, then perhaps you were not the right person to be in the job..

In light of this, I found I resisted talking about how I was feeling and kept all the questions I was asking myself, buried in my mind. I became my own worst judge about how well or not I could do each job. Despite my manager and colleagues telling me that I was progressing well in my abilities, my first experience of a patient dying in my care before I could get them to a hospital, left me extremely shocked and with a mind in an overdrive of questions that I didn't have answers to.

As I withdrew more into these unanswered questions, I found it had become a spiral of over thinking about the next job and the next. How could I do another job that didn't fit the script of what we had been taught? How would this person's family feel about paramedics now? Would they blame me? Would my work partner on the day ever be able to trust me again? Would others find out I was not good enough to do the job? What had I missed? What didn't I understand about what was happening? I was alone in my thoughts and hurting deeply by the uncertainty and fear of my own lack of understanding. This overflowed into my personal life when I couldn't find the words to tell my family and friends what I was feeling, and I began to pull away from them and retreat more and more into my own mind space.

One day the questions overwhelmed my brain and I found myself cowering in a teary mess and unable to answer the next job call. I was taken off the road for a while, and in the days at home alone I then felt isolated and angry. I got physically sick from the overload of stress, and my circle of support diminished as I pushed people further away. I could no longer leave my house on my own and it became a haven of solitude. Home was a place to hide from the eyes of the world and lick the wounds that had cut so deep. There was no enjoyment in the activities I had once enjoyed, and my mind chatter was so loud that it blocked the ability to study or find any peace. In the deepest inky black of the worst days of what was diagnosed as job-specific PTSD, I could only see a bleak and dark future. It was on one of these dismal mornings that I attempted to end my own life. In a twist of irony, that was not to be my fate that day.

The sequence of events that occurred in that very desolate moment started me on the slow process of recovery. I needed time to talk about the job and how it had made me feel, then to self-reflect and begin to integrate what I found in the jumbled mass of thoughts that job had prompted.

It took loads of soul searching,professional help and support to decide if I could continue in my chosen profession. Was I too vulnerable? Was I too weak? Was I too caring and unable to separate my emotions? Would I ever feel well or smile again? Did I have the ability to make good decisions? Did I trust myself and my colleagues enough to open up and ask for help if I needed it? Was I a good enough person? All the questions any of us ask ourselves when the things in our life don't go to plan and begin to crumble.

One thing I never ever questioned though was my passion and love for the job, and my resolve to go on and be the best paramedic I could be. Being so early in my career I had not yet had the chance to feel I had achieved this. My dream was still alive and it remained a powerful force in my recovery .

In time I became fully conscious that all I had learned as a student was only the preamble of what this job was in its entirety. If I was to continue as a paramedic it would take a higher level of self awareness, confidence and resilience to return to the job I loved. I would need to build a trust in my workmates and to share my feelings without fear. Finding my own ability to stand tall, and allow forgiveness towards myself for faltering was the start of the healing. I had to start over and accept that I was a novice and had a lot more to learn. It was like learning to ride a bike, you fall off and skin your knees and it hurts for a while, but even with the fear of more pain you get back on and ride again until you master the task.

I think many of us go through life wondering if we are good enough to do the jobs we are doing. Waiting for the moment when we are found out and seen to be lacking or not being enough. This is a common syndrome called Imposter Syndrome which is a fear of being found out for not being good enough.

https://en.wikipedia.org/wiki/Impostor_syndrome
https://qz.com/984070/neil-gaiman-has-the-perfect-anecdote-for-anyone-with-impostors-syndrome/

Many nights I lay awake wondering if I was good enough to be able to do this job I had chosen. This became another choice point in my life. I could leave my job, start again and do something else, or I could go back to my job with the new wisdom I had acquired and bring the dream back to life. My only other option was to stay in thedarkness that had enveloped me, and become a diminished and sad version of myself.

The dream was still too strong and even though the vision had faded, I knew I could bring the colour back. There was no other choice for me - I went back to work.

We all hit rough and rocky patches during this journey called life. Here are a few tips that helped me through one of those times when the road was not so smooth.

Learnings from this chapter...

1. We all have the fear of what we do not understand. Never be afraid to seek help, ask questions and keep asking until you know the answer.
2. Imposter syndrome is a normal affliction of the human mind. Many of us feel that we are not good enough, but it is just a feeling. Thoughts and beliefs can be changed by seeking out and changing our ideas of the way we see things.
3. When it gets too hard, ask for help.

—— CHAPTER 7 ——

HEALING AND GROWTH

"Never be afraid to start again, it is the chance to build a better version of yourself."
Stephanie Altus

Can you imagine moving away from all you know to a whole new place and starting over? Have you ever wanted something so badly, that you are prepared to go the extra mile to make it happen? Do you know what it feels like to triumph over tragedy?

Once the choice to go back to work was made, it was not going to be an easy or straight forward process and I would have to make some hard decisions.

My family and closest friends had never left my side during that grey and dismal time, and been my constant support and my greatest advocates. They trusted me enough to know that I would do what was right for me, to find the power to rebuild my dream career. I also had much support and help from two amazing mentors who had stayed by my side through this whole painful episode. The biggest thing they did for me was to hold me accountable for my own decisions and provide encouragement to rise again and move forward. They didn't allow me to become a victim, rather ensured I took responsibility to own my part in all that had occurred. They guided me as I let go of the anger towards others, who I felt had not supported me.

To get back to work and truely have a fresh start, I made the toughest decision of all. With everything that had happened as a result of this bout of PTSD it was too difficult return to work in the location where this job had happened. I felt like my colleagues there had defined me by the PTSD, and had forgotten that behind that diagnosis was a strong and multifaceted woman who had survived more than one tough life moment. Being around the people who judged me as "suffering from PSTD", I found myself reacting to them as that "PTSD person". Out of frustration and anger, I was making poor choices in my behaviour because I felt I had no voice to stand up for myself yet and fight their opinions. I struggled due to the fact I still identified with the persona that was made up of the symptoms of PTSD, and I allowed myself to shrink back when I couldn't explain what I was feeling.

Slowly though, I healed and reconnected with my life outside of the work environment, and returned to the person I had been before PTSD. Gradually I went back to doing the things I loved, like walking on the beach and spending time with my friends. I wasn't able to face crowds and still had panic attacks when I was overwhelmed by tasks that put me out of my comfort zone. And I still felt small and timid in the face of my work colleagues who had seen me in that broken state.

Not everyone was supportive of my return to work, and many days it seemed almost impossible to break the stigma and opinions of those who would never have the ability to really listen and hear the truth of why I knew I could still be a good paramedic. Those who have not had the experience of PTSD would never be able to understand that it is a diagnosis, not the entire person.

One day, after yet another confrontation with one of my colleagues who was pushing me to resign, I felt like I had finally been backed into a corner. Have you ever considered how you would feel if you are backed into a corner with no escape and the fear of feeling threatened? Like the boxer in the ring who is forced to the corner and can either cower or fight, I came out fighting. I earnestly explored every possible way of bringing this dream back to life without the constant feeling of being in the dark shadow of PTSD. I was not going to break apart and fall again.

A paramedic job vacancy opened up in another location far from where I wasworking. Here, I could go and start over in a place where people didn't know me. I could go back into the job and just be myself. I applied and got the position.

I packed up my home and life as I knew it up till that point and left to start anew. This location was 900km away in a place I knew absolutely nothing about, and had little idea of where it even was.

In the instant of saying goodbye to my now grown up girls, I almost stopped and gave up on my dream. I had never been so far away from my daughters before. They were my life and everything that mattered most to me, but I knew I must take a risk, take a chance and give this dream my best shot. If it still didn't work out, I would then know that I had tried my absolute best and would have no regrets if I had to leave the job.

Do you know what it is like to leave everything you know and love to move to an unknown place that seems a whole world away? Many people actually do this by moving to another country. Here I was, moving to the other side of the state and it felt like I was about to enter a foreign land.

Having never been to this place before, I had no home to move to, no friends there and no idea if I would even like the place or not. As I drove over, my car filled with the only possessions I could take with me, tears streamed down my face and apprehension filled my gut. This decision seemed to have a touch of craziness to it. Every kilometre I drove took me further and further from all that was familiar and comforting to me, and I wondered if the fear of losing my dream was less than the fear of metaphorically leaping from this cliff I had just jumped off. Despite this, I knew in my heart that no matter what happened with my job in this new place, I would build my wings and fly, and eventually I would soar again on the currents of success.

I didn't know the roads I was travelling, or if I was going in the right direction. My phone had no service to ring and talk to my daughters for reassurance, and I wondered how in the world I was going to make this work. Having no home to go to when I arrived, I had booked a cabin at the local caravan park, so at least when I arrived I would have somewhere to stay.

As I drove further and further, I began to get clarity that this decision was more than just about keeping the dream alive. It was about expanding my awareness and building a stronger resilience and hardiness in myself. It was about learning to survive without all my default comforts. It was being open to new experiences and exploring new places. It was choosing to trust myself, despite my doubts, apprehension, fear and the multitude of unknowns.

Finally I arrived, and as I drove into this little town I was exhausted and drained of all energy and enthusiasm. I booked straight into the caravan park and headed to the little cabin that was awaiting me. Unpacking my meager possessions, I was overwhelmed by the enormity of what I had just embarked upon. I rang my daughters and, with the strength I didn't feel, I put excitement into my voice and conversation to assure them I was ok and that this was going to be an exciting adventure. When I hung up I prepared my uniform for the morning, set my alarm, lay down and sobbed hot wretched tears into my pillow until I fell asleep.

Sleep that night was fitful at best and in the morning I resolved to change my attitude and be grateful that I even had this choice. I decided not to feel sorry for myself but to make this time and place an adventure to be curiously explored. It would be like a holiday, filled with the wonder of finding new treasures in the area and meeting new people along the way. I smiled, got up, got dressed, and had a coffee on the verandah of my cabin.

In the cloud that had surrounded me on my arrival the night before, I had not noticed that my cabin overlooked the beautiful bay of the ocean and was surrounded by native trees filled with a variety of birdlife. After coffee, it was time to go and start my first day of the job in this new area.

Arriving at work I felt that familiar sense of apprehension, however I had now decided to embrace it and replace it with the excitement of meeting new people who may later become friends. I started the rebuilding of my dream.

The initial days back at work were difficult because of my own doubt, and knowing that not everyone agreed with my decision, or believed that I could overcome the PTSD and be a competent and happy paramedic once again. At this point I made a choice that I was going to prove a point to all the doubters that they were wrong. For the most part, my time in this new place was happy and successful. I kept in contact with my mentors throughout my time away, and valued the support, accountability and encouragement that was provided.

Proving a point is an interesting way of coping with negative feedback and I discovered that this was a method that I had used many times previously when I felt others didn't have faith in my ability. If anyone expressed to me that I was unable to achieve something I wanted to do, their words would cause my feelings to be wounded and I would feel pained by their opinion. As a result I would go out and attempt to do exactly what they thought I couldn't, as a method to move away from the pain I perceived they had caused by doubting me.

In reality this was actually an internal pain of feeling that I was not good enough to achieve my goals, and my lack of taking action while working towards my goals. In each instance this had happened, I discovered that proving a point started to fade over time as I began to enjoy what I was doing and continued to achieve the goals for my own happiness and reward. Once I got to the moment of doing it for myself, I started taking action towards the pleasure of the results I was getting.

Soon, working at this new station and reconstructing my career filled me with the same immense joy I had felt in my student days. I was enjoying the job more and more and over the following years, I worked my way from being a novice to being competent.

I was engaged with the team I worked with, and I trusted them to share my experiences and feelings along the way. In turn they shared their stories with me, they embraced and supported me, and introduced me to all the beauty and culture of the area. They taught me where all the main geographical areas were, and over the coming weeks I began to explore further and further afield.

Being on my own was no longer a sad and fearful time. Instead it became a time to embrace the solitude and use the time to try new things that I had longed to explore. I spent my days in wonder and curiosity, filling the alone times with seeing the sights and getting involved in community events and groups. Every day I still missed my girls, but I gained skills in self-sufficiency and courage that would bode well long into my future. From this new aspect of my career I found the person I wanted to define myself as being, while attaining my dream of being a successful paramedic. And it was here in this place I found exactly that.

I now knew that my own vulnerability, my passion and joy in the job was greater than it had ever been. I no longer feared that I would be found lacking in my ability and began assisting the students with their learning. From having known the darkness of PTSD, I applied a balance to my work and personal life and imparted to others the importance of not allowing work to become your only identity. I was getting well again and the nightmares and constant mind chatter had eased. I eventually came to a point where I knew I could return to my previous work location without shame or fear.

I waited patiently for a position to be advertised in my dream location and when it came up, applied without hesitation. I was going to miss this bunch of colleagues who had helped to pick me up and take me from broken to healed, but I was going home. Back to my family and friends, with my dream once again intact and as a vibrant and more confident version of myself.

My return came with a new vision and goal in place. My intention was to work in my dream location and finish my career there by retiring as a respected paramedic. I no longer held aspirations to achieve anything more than just giving my best to every patient I attended and enjoying my job. I was satisfied to have survived PTSD and still be passionate about my work.

In finishing, when I started in my role as a paramedic, I had never heard of or considered PTSD, and had little understanding or knowledge of what the experience of it would be like. I missed all the warning signs of my own deterioration into it and by the time I sought help, was already in a bad place in my mind. The whole experience of it was a tragic and colossal time of falling into a dark and self-destructive tunnel of recurring nightmares and ominous thoughts. I was able to heal through receiving loads of support, as well as learning much about myself and other people. Eventually I came to an acceptance of the fact that we all see life and the world from our own perceptions, and we are all so much more than the one-dimensional impression we have of ourselves and others when we only see them from one facet.

Learnings from this chapter...

1. You can rebuild a dream if the passion is still there. When all seems lost, with courage, support and reflection you can become a better version of you and become the person you need to be to recreate your success.

2. This chapter highlights the benefits of working with a mentor or coach by your side because your family and friends are there to be that, your family and friends. They are your constant and your greatest allies and will have your back even when you falter. The beauty of having a coach or mentor is that they're not meant to be your friend, they're not meant to please you. They are going to give you tough love, and to hold you accountable for your own actions. This is the secret and most important ingredient for success when you need someone to guide you.

3. Take risks and embrace change. Sometimes the scariest things you do can lead you to new and exciting experiences.

4. When you have a decision to make, you can either stay stuck or move forward. Sometimes this may be taking the tiniest of steps forward or taking a giant leap. Either way, just keep moving.

EXPANDING AND SUCCESS

"Small opportunities can be the chance to learn unexpected and exciting new things."
Stephanie Altus

Opportunities are sometimes presented to us at the most unexpected times. We have decided on the path we intend to take and feel content in where we are headed. Then someone sees more potential in us than we see in ourselves and we find ourselves being offered the chance to do something we had never before considered. It can also change the course of our journey into the future.

Moving home to work in my dream location filled my mind with happy thoughts of a beautiful home where my family would come for frequent and regular visits, having friends to socialise with and share fun times, and working with people I had known and got on well with prior to the whole PTSD saga.

It was an area I knew well and loved, close to the beach with a relaxed and happy environment. I was excited and exhilarated with the thought that I was adding the final touch to my long held dream and this was the extra sparkle that would complete it. I felt like I had come full circle and I would be heading towards retirement in the place I had begun, with the joy and passion I had started my career with all those years ago in my volunteer days.

Again, I underestimated how rocky even the road to paradise can be. I returned to a very different team than the one I had left a few years before. My favourite colleagues had also been through many life changes in the time I was away, which meant the ease and comfort of familiar relationships was no longer there. Routines had altered and the cohesion and team times I had previously loved, had ceased to exist.

My return was marred by an event at work which placed a shadow over my coming home. At first I felt disconnected and betrayed by those I had previously trusted. In a misunderstanding of communication, I had returned to a space of withdrawal and isolation. Hesitation and uncertainty about my decision to move back was a constant fear for my first few weeks. Balanced out by a feeling of certainty for my love of the job and confidence in my ability to do it, I was able to work with professionalism and ensure that each and every job received my full attention.

Outside of work my life was settled and happy and I loved being home with my daughters close by. My time spent with them and my granddaughter more than made up for the disappointment of the lack-lustre return to my dream work location.

The weeks passed by and I gradually established a new rapport with my colleagues, my job became equally as happy as my home life. Now I had achieved the ultimate dream complete with the glitter - my dream job, in my perfect location, with colleagues I got on well with and we could share a laugh and have fun. Over time, I put the past of PTSD behind me and it no longer felt like a part of who I was.

I had often heard people say "If only I could ..." or, "When I reach........this or that will happen". Many times I had said it myself, "When I succeed in my dream job and work in my dream location, I will be truly happy and not need anything more". But this is often a false sense of reality. People either never get to that utopian moment or, once they do, they become stagnant and bored and the stirrings of finding a new challenge or dream to add begin to emerge. Maybe a bigger and better opportunity presents to them which they cannot refuse, or life suddenly changes and their utopia is shattered. Life is never a linear path and none of us can ever know what the next moment may hold for us.

Having reached my own Nirvana, I became complacent in my thoughts and relaxed more and more into the blasé sense of being safe and protected by this Teflon coating of having experienced PTSD in the past and recovering from it. I would never allow it to happen to me again, and I now knew how to protect myself from the over questioning and mind chatter that had haunted me after each job.. I had seen enough of the trauma and devastation of life through my work that I believed I could manage anything else that this job threw at me, and if I did go to a scene that rattled me, I would be able to recognise the signs early and ask for help before it became a problem.

During this time of contentment and having it all, a position became vacant at work to act as a relief manager to cover holiday leave. It was suggested to me that I should apply for the role. This was not something I had contemplated since prior to experiencing the PTSD, even though I had done a few short stints in a similar role earlier in my career, I was unsure if I was capable of doing it, but decided to take the risk. I applied and was appointed to the position.

This was a whole new sphere added to my career. Once again I had the opportunity to learn new skills and stretch my boundaries and grow into this new role. Having a mentor was even more important in stepping up, because now I was not only dealing with unknown people and personalities on cases, I was also dealing with the personalities and demands of my colleagues and the job from a management perspective.

So many lessons were presented to me in this new position and I took on each one with enthusiasm. Now I aspired to lead my team by being the best example I could, both in my on-road position and that of the team leader. Once again, I loved the challenge that this new aspect to the job provided, and loved both the management role and personal growth that was occurring at the time. The sparkle in my dream job now had a gold-tinted edge. Never had I imagined that this would be the track I would be following as I edged closer to retirement.

It was more rewarding now to look back on where I had come from and see all that I had overcome to get to this place. I was both in awe and terrified of the responsibility of looking after my team than ever before.

Gradually, I learned how to feel the discomfort but still rise to every new test that was put in front of me. It was a case of Feel the Fear and do it anyway – and there's a book with that title that I recommend reading if you are contemplating a new challenge but feel fearful of doing it.

As I became more familiar with the tasks the job required and gained proficiency in undertaking them, I began to be given more and more responsibility. At times I felt motivated and enthused by the extra tasks, but at other times I felt overwhelmed by the enormity of the next step I had to conquer.

As a naturally caring and compassionate person, a trait I had never lost through the tribulation of PTSD, I often went above what was expected to provide support and assistance to my team members when it was needed. Seeing the job from this new outlook meant I was now able to see how much work it was and how and why many decisions were made, even when it made no sense to the team. I had the benefit of seeing the box from multiple perspectives and nothing was as simple as it seemed.

When I stepped down from the role I was able to slot back easily into my on-road position.. I felt like I now had the best of two worlds, that of a paramedic and the option to step up and lead my team. I knew that I would never apply to take this role on a full-time basis, due to the intensity of added stress it involved. I knew myself well enough to understand that I was not cut out to take on every facet that a management role required, but I was happy doing the relief role in short bursts.

The next couple of years whizzed by so fast and I was living life in this comfortable routine where I felt like

I had progressed from being competent to being proficient in my job. I had achieved a nice balance between my work and personal life. I was enjoying being a paramedic, with the constant unknown of what we might do next, and the benefits my work life provided, and trying out many new and fun things on my days off. I was loving all of the enjoyment life had to offer.

One day I noticed that a few small cracks had appeared on the smooth surface I had been navigating. The universe had started to throw a few curve balls my way and, at the outset, I was capable of catching them and throwing back each one. Soon, they started coming more rapidly and more than one at a time, and eventually I was struggling to catch them individually anymore. So began the juggling act of trauma, tragedy and heartache that was to eventually overcome my coping mechanisms once more.

This became the worst year I had ever experienced in the job since starting as a volunteer some 20 years ago. It was a year of attending the worst jobs I had ever seen in my career, one stacked upon the next in a relentless stream of trauma and sadness. Coupled with the serious illness, injury and deaths of a number of my family, friends and colleagues over that 12-month period, the disbelief, grief and pain were forming more and more layers around me with each event.

The run of devastating jobs were taking a toll on some of my team, and I had a lack of experience to help them in the way they most needed. It was not one job that caused distress for everyone, rather different aspects of a culmination of cases. Seeking assistance to guide the team, I was offered options and presented them to those that required it. These were often seen as unpalatable and rejected.

The stress of the management role had now started to take its toll, not only was I trying to address and support my team members through these jobs and their own personal traumas, I was also trying to cope my own reactions to the events that were occurring.

For me, it was one job - in one moment, on one day - that changed everything!

This was the first time I felt real fear and terror when attending a scene. It was the job that no matter how much I tried, I just could not integrate it into my mind. All my values and beliefs about life were challenged on that day. It all seemed to happen so fast, yet time stood still. The confusion, the chaos, the trauma and the tragedy were of a level that I couldn't comprehend. Compounded by the effect this job had on my workmates who were also there, this job became the unbearable tasking. There was no time to process or debrief the job before another trauma case was dispatched to us, and we needed to move our focus onto another new scene. By the time we finished late that night, everyone who had been at the previous job had already gone home. The moment to debrief and start to understand all that had happened was lost!

The run of distressing jobs seemed relentless through the rest of the year and I had learned to stop questioning the why of each situation so that I could turn up for work and keep doing the next job and the next one and the next one...

At that specific time I didn't feel the enormity of the strain of increasing pressure. I shared a few of these experiences with my family and workmates and as a precautionary measure, I started to see the psychologist I had seen during the previous bout of PTSD.

Despite the run of traumatic cases we were attending, our team pulled together to support each other. I noticed an increase in the black humour and minor changes in the behaviour of some my workmates and myself, but I had no idea that the pressure cooker of stress and emotion in the team was about to blow up.

As I watched my workmates begin to fragment and fall, I increasingly felt the distress of what we had experienced. At the time I had little recall or specific memory of that one job and had done a good job of pushing the horror of what I had seen into a locked recess in my mind.

Most deeply I was feeling the defeat and failure of not being able to comfort and aide my team members to recovery from the traumatic memories these jobs were creating. I was the team leader and it was my role to lead by example and assist my team to seek and accept the help they so clearly needed. How was I to do this with any effect when I was with them at these jobs and alternate support was sadly lacking at that time? Or maybe, as previously, there was still a perceived culture to not speak up and admit so many were struggling with their thoughts. Instead we all chose to keep going, to soldier on until we had no more to give.

It was Christmas Eve of that same year when the final blow was struck. I had been looking forward to going home to be with my waiting family. It was our annual Christmas tradition to share a roast dinner and watch the carols on the television. Almost at knock off time the pager went off and, reading the job on the screen, I instantly knew that I was going to be absent from those celebrations.

This was another traumatic job that proved to be a difficult and prolonged tasking that took a final toll on me. It was only the second time in my career that I had felt unsafe on a job. As I was finishing with tidying up the scene and putting the kits into the ambulance, I felt angry and wondered what I was doing here in this place on Christmas Eve instead of being at home with those I loved.

On returning home, I went straight to the shower. Once I was changed I joined my girls on the couch, but I was unable to talk with them about where I had been for so long. That night the nightmares started, and a rush of emotion which I seemed unable to stem, flowed through me. The floodgates had opened and there was no holding it back. I rapidly spiraled into a dark and murky whirlpool of emotion, recalled events and an anger that was not going to easily be suppressed. I had missed too many important moments with my family, seen too many things that no person should have to see, worked in every conceivable adverse weather condition in both day and night hours, looked after others and given compassion to every patient in my care. I had nothing left on this night. After only a few weeks, I was taken off of the road again due to PTSD and burnout. It was to be a long time before I would wear my uniform again.

Learnings from this chapter...

1. This chapter has talks of the highest moment of exhilaration and how that can easily turn and become the worst of life's moments.
2. Happy times and sad times do not last. Life is a constant ebb and flow of good and bad times.
3. We never really get to a point where we are finished learning. The school of life is an ever-evolving journey of lessons that teach us, if we are willing to learn.
4. If life is hard, take the time to stop and seek all the help you need. DO NOT be afraid to speak up and admit you are not doing ok.
5. Practice self-care first. You cannot help others for long if you are actively bleeding from your own wounds.

CRACKS BECOME CHASMS

"It is always darkest before the dawn."
Stephanie Altus

As an emergency services worker, people often ask you "What is the worst thing you have ever seen in your job?" Try imagining the worst ever horror movie you have ever seen and then times it by an unlimited number. That would be the worst I've ever seen and then more. The longer you remain in a job where you deal daily with human suffering, the more worst jobs you accumulate in your memories. After almost 25 years, the list of the most terrible things I have seen still grows. Even now, I can be caught off guard by suffering and trauma of people I see when working in my role.

When you ask me this question, you are asking me to relive the most horrific moments of my life. You know I cannot answer you! I do not want to put you through even the idea of my reality, and many of the things we see must remain unspoken due to maintaining a sensitivity to the confidentiality of those involved.

This chapter is a raw and personal account of what PTSD was like for me. Not everyone who has had (or is suffering from) PTSD will experience it like I did, but most people who know the anguish of this diagnosis will find similarities.

If you are reading this chapter and identify with any of the information or have difficulty after reading the content, please seek help from either a health professional or contact beyondblue https://www.beyondblue.org.au/ or Lifeline on 131114 *https://www.lifeline.org.au*

It is said that our brain can only take in seven to eight new pieces of information at any one time. https://en.wikipedia.org/wiki/The_Magical_Number_Seven,_Plus_or_Minus_Two

In the role of a paramedic we are often faced with an overwhelming amount of information on every job. As we progress through each case, we sift out what we need and the rest is filed into the memory bank of our brain to be forgotten unless we need it, or an event at a later time triggers remembrance. It is a unique and novel role that we play, often in uncontrolled environments that contain chaos and confusion. Our job is to come in and restore some calm, while providing the essential care and treatment that is needed.

When we go to some of these jobs, the stimulation of sensory overabundance means that we rapidly push information into the black boxes of our minds so we can focus fully on the care of the patient. The seven to eight spaces for new information are taken up with listening to what has happened, attending to the patient's needs, deciding on the treatment required and how to best care and management for each patient.

There is no time to take in the confusion of the broken pieces on a scene, the emotions, the screams, the flashing lights, the weather, your own need to eat or go to the toilet. The moment becomes frozen in a flurry of activity which is centered on patient care. And this is as it should be, this is what we are trained to do.

Over the years, as we gain experience in our jobs, many of the tasks become automated and we can do them without too much thinking. Like driving a car, at first it is hard and you have to think about every small aspect of the task. Then after a few years of driving, most people can drive while listening to the radio or having a conversation. As time goes on they begin to notice more and more around them and can respond more rapidly to sudden and unexpected changes.

The same can be said for any career. The longer you hold a position, the easier it becomes to perform the job without taking notice of every small detail. When you arrive at this level of expertise, a quick glance can take in an abundance of information and the mind is left free to focus on only the more difficult tasks. The things you notice in those first moments are not forgotten, but rather stored in the deeper recesses of our brains.

When I started in this job, there were so many things to learn. The college taught the things we needed to do our jobs safely and to the best benefit of each patient we would encounter. We learned the skills we needed, the knowledge that supported the skills, how to use the equipment, how to save a life, administration requirements, how to access help if you needed it after a job, self-care techniques, policies and procedures, emergency driving and radio procedure. They took us through simulations of cases we might attend and showed us pictures from news reports, of a few of the scenes we might see. They taught us about managing a scene and how to create some order from disorder and the lecturers could describe some of the jobs they had been to themselves. This job requires many, many aspects of skill to provide a safe and beneficial service to patients and the wider community.

What we could never learn from the college was what stress feels like for you as an individual. What are the unique warning signs and triggers we might feel. They could not recreate the people, their emotions and personalities, and carnage of a real scene. They could not teach us the overwhelm of the senses when they are being over stimulated by the multitude of things happening simultaneously. They could not teach us how to feel when we could not save a life, despite our very best efforts, or how to tell a patient's loved one that we did the best we could.

By nature, the job of a paramedic is to save lives and we pride ourselves on how we do our jobs. No one but others in these same types of jobs can tell you the impact of going from patient to patient, often without a break, and the mind shift that needs to occur between each one. No one can tell you that you need to have a bladder the size of a giant because you may not get near a toilet for hours, or that you need to have a cast iron stomach to deal with the array of bodily elements you will encounter. You cannot teach of the adaptability and flexibility you need when circumstances change suddenly, or of the compassion you will feel when a job tugs at your heart-strings.

The life of a paramedic is unpredictable and extreme and this is both the excitement and emotion of the job. In one moment you can be treating an elderly woman having chest pain, and the next moment you are comforting a teenager while trying to save the life of the friend they just killed when they crashed the car. You can go from the uncontrollable seizing baby whose mother is screaming with fear, straight to a very elderly year person that you know you are taking from their home for the last time while their lifelong very elderly spouse cries for a life that will never be the same. You may attend the regular caller who has had a toothache for the past month and has run out of panadol tonight, right before attending the young woman who is losing her baby due to a miscarriage. You see the carnage of death in traffic accidents and the vile and disgusting injuries humans inflict on others in moments of rage. Each and every patient confronts you with the worst moment they are experiencing for them right in that space in time.

Some say this is what you take on when you sign up to do the job. True enough! What they fail to remember, is that none of us know how we will feel or react in any situation unless we have experienced it. Even then each time we see any event, we react in our own individual way, dependent on all the contributing factors in that exact time.

How can you know right now, what you would feel if you were faced with the worst thing you had ever seen, and it was beyond your scope of understanding at that time? How can you say that your reaction will be the same each and every time, when so many factors can alter any moment?

Humans are an interesting group. We all have a mind full of memories of all the moments of our lives. We acknowledge, accept and celebrate the good memories and the emotions they provoke. I have a beautiful memory of being a child in my grandparents' garden. It was filled with flowers and trees surrounding a soft green lawn. All through the garden that surrounded the lawn was a meandering pathway that had secret spots to sit and while away the time. I loved nothing better than to swing on the big swing at the edge of the lawn, before wandering these paths to pick a bunch of flowers to take in to grandma. Whenever I smell a Gardenia in bloom now, my mind is instantly transported back to those carefree days of a child's wonder.

However, when our memory triggers back to horrible or unfavourable moments we have experienced, we are taught by society that they are bad and we feel pressured to shut them downand not speak of them, for fear of the disgust it will cause others if we tell of it.

PTSD for me was an insidious disorder. It crept up silently and it wasn't until it had a firm hold that I could identify its clutches. When I look back now, I can see the early signs that were not clearly evident at the time. The blocking out of memories of jobs I had been to, restless sleep, an increase in my reflex responses if someone or something happened suddenly, emotions that were becoming more unstable, a loss of trust in anyone but myself, withdrawal and an increase in drinking alcohol after my shifts. Relationships became strained and friends were pushed further away as my tolerance and concentration levels fell, and I could no longer tolerate noise. Television became a trigger for the traumatic memories, as it is filled with shows that depict the terror of the things I had seen. A sense of failure grew and secrets were kept to protect others and myself. I stopped talking and started to become more isolated.

This was the second time I had been diagnosed with PTSD, but this time the added burden of burnout and job fatigue accompanied my tortured mind. The first diagnosis of PTSD was due to a single job. One was a job that had caused confusion and conflict of nothing making sense, combined with a death I didn't expect at the start of the job and the dynamics created when conflict occurs between two colleagues on a case. This time however, it was to be a cumulative PTSD from the multitude of jobs I had done in my 20 years of service. And the rawness it left me with, was to change who I would become, ways I could never foresee in those early days of being diagnosed.

When you work in emergency service or any type of job where you see stuff that you cannot comprehend fully at the time, the memories get pushed to the back of your mind and build on each other. They continue to stack up and get pushed back further and further into the deep memory cells in our brain. One day, for whatever reason, the little black box that holds all those stored memories of what you've seen, breaks open. Now, instead of just one job, it becomes flashbacks of all the jobs you have ever seen. Each memory prompts another, and soon the film contains a rerun of each and every case you have ever done, even the simplest ones. Your senses become increasingly heightened and the smallest of triggers can set off a replay of any or all the scenes from your motion picture. Sleep does not protect you from seeing all that you want to forget, and the nightmares are so real, you think you have returned back in time to the moment each job happened. Sleep deprivation soon becomes a normal part of how you live.

PTSD can occur for so many reasons; it may be due to the busyness of the job and the fact that you didn't have time to think about one case prior to going to the next. It might be the lack of ability to integrate everything that's going on in a job or that you have reached the level of your skill set and cannot provide the patient with the extra they need. There may be something in the job that causes you to feel extreme danger and fear, or it might be that you can relate to the job and you empathise to deeply. Your individual values or coping mechanisms play a role and the level of support you receive at the time or in the days after can have a large impact. The connection with your colleagues is important, as is getting validation that your feelings are ok. Perhaps it is that you've hit the boundaries of your experience and exposure and can no longer understand what is happening. Jobs that clash and coexist with what's happening in your own life at the time have a larger impact. Doing multiple jobs one on top of the other, over a very short space of time and fatigue increase the risk. The morale of your team and leadership in your workplace could be lacking, or stereotyping and culture can prevent you asking for help. When you feel unable to access adequate support that meets your needs, it compounds the sense of failure exponentially.

So, what I experienced as PTSD, was an inability to process the overwhelming and conflicting emotions I experienced on that one highly traumatizing job, combined with no time to stop before the next traumatic job was dispatched and the lack of support in the immediate days after. This was a shift which had too many detrimental factors, and a job that I had never, ever imagined as a possibility of attending.

PTSD is something that is almost impossible to describe to someone who has never experienced it. It is a nightmare of reliving cases as if they are happening in that very moment, along with all the fear and emotion that was suppressed at the time of the jobs. You feel alone, isolated and unable to find the words to tell others what is happening in your brain. You doubt your own thoughts and try to shut them down. It becomes a constant battle to survive what is already past, but your mind won't let you forget.

For anyone who works in these careers, we go out every day to do our best; to save lives, and create some order and certainty for each patient, and those around them, in their moment of distress. What happens though, when we can no longer do this for ourselves? How do you convey what these memories are like? How do you speak of what you have seen? Imagine for a moment watching a movie that contains a thousand scenes that you would rather forget.

In the life of a paramedic, every shift is filled with jobs that have the potential to cause distress. Jobs that took you minutes or hours, in the heat, rain or hail! Every case where you work under the scrutiny of a loved one, the general public or worse, in view of the whole world as the media flash cameras on what should be the most private of moments. Jobs that are in locations that are difficult to access or in the most filth-ridden place you have ever seen. The jobs that make you want to take a shower immediately after, to wash off the heat, dust, body fluids, smells, grime and your own sweat. Or the job that you arrive at and soon realise that this patient is your loved one or a friend.

We choose this job because it is our passion and it is what we want to do. It is a job that we love and we give our all on each and every shift. There are the days when you're acutely aware that your family is missing you, while you are out caring for others but you know that every patient needs what you can provide. But it is this same job that you love, which can take you to a place of darkness and burnout, leaving you unable to perform even the simplest task.

PTSD can be due to one job or an accumulation of jobs, I have had both. I have had the one job that I could resolve and get back to work, and I have had the accumulation of more than 20 years of jobs.

That one big job that started the slide into this world of accumulative PTSD and changed my view of life as I then knew it, challenged my ability to integrate what I had seen into my reality of the world. It was a big job that lasted a long time, and made no sense to me through the confusion that confronted us on the scene. It was the job that heightened all my senses and made me feel a gut-filled fear. The whole time I was acutely hyper-reactive inside my mind, while outwardly showing a sense of calm. Too much happened too quickly and, before the paperwork was even complete, the next was on our screen.

The ability to move rapidly in ever changing and dynamic situations is part of the everyday experiences of a paramedic. It becomes a natural instinct as you move further into your career and you gain the ability to notice the subtle things that make you aware that all is not as it seems. PTSD creates an over-exaggerated version of this response and you become hyper aware and hyper vigilant. Your stress response is in constant overdrive, even when you are no longer at work. Slight and sudden movements or occurrences can send the adrenaline rush into an acute over abundance. You begin to get jittery and fidgety and it gets harder to relax. Over time, you become less and less able to cope with places that stimulate your senses. Even a trip to the shop becomes an almost unbearable task.

For me, PTSD seemed like a dark cloud that obscured my instinct and ability to make choices in moments of tension. My brain struggled to find any answers to the never ending questions in life; from even the simplest, like what milk to buy, to the most complex.

Being a paramedic requires rapid action when a patient's life hangs in the balance and they sit there on that precipice of life. They depend on the correctness of your actions and decisions. Instinctively you need to do what you have been taught to do to save a life. So when the answers no longer came easily, I had no option but stop being at work.

My emotions increasingly became raw and flickered from one to another in an uncontrolled manner. It seems that my ability to be the graceful swan floating on the pond while paddling underneath the water had ceased to exist. I had now become the floundering fish on the bank of the river, flipping about in a desperate attempt to get back into the depths of the river currents so that I could breathe normally again.

As my thoughts became darker and darker, my world closed in around me. Sleep eluded me, to be replaced by nightmares more horrific than any of the events I had seen. Reality clashed with illusion and I no longer knew or understood how to interpret what I was experiencing. It was in these moments that my only desire was to numb the constant horror that fatigued me. I turned to alcohol and medication just to allow my mind to stop for what seemed like only seconds. As I spiralled down into the well of cold icy blackness, I could no longer socialise with even those closest to me. A once vibrant and passionate human, I had become a crusted and cracking empty vessel.

I could not see even a short distance into the future, was required to answer questions and explain what I did not yet understand to my work. I didn't yet have answers, couldn't concentrate and my mind was like a train out of control down a hillside. My constant companion became anger directed at an unseen and unknown target – no one was to blame, but yet I wanted to blame everyone and everything.

Mostly though, there was a sense of hopelessness that the never ending rerun of jobs in my mind would never end. I could not control it despite always having been the one in control. I felt the hopelessness for voiceless and faceless person I thought I had become and for the hurt and pain I both felt and was causing my family.

Hopelessness is a dangerous outcrop to sit on. From here every moment is a choice point - to remain seated there or throw yourself off the edge. Even the slightest movement in any direction can become the catalyst for falling further.

As you sit still and alone, thoughts of death start to intrude into the never ending avalanche of images in your mind. The stillness and peace of 'no longer existing' feels like the only way out and you feel in your heart that those you love would have less pain in the grief of death than what you think you are causing them now.

I began to draw pictures of what PTSD was like for me. My first was a picture of me, falling into a muddy river and being engulfed by the filthy current of water, my body being dragged down by the dark sludge. And I remember the feeling I felt while I drew it, of my body filling with the slime till I could no longer breath, the coldness of the water slowing my heart beat, and continuing until it had filled every cell and my soul began to die.

I drew many pictures in those days of PTSD. It was easier to show it in a picture than speak the words. And I began to write the thoughts I couldn't say out loud. Through all these days and weeks and months, and despite the depths of pain and fear and raw emotion, my girls and my granddaughter walked beside me. Never once wavering in their love and support, and without judgement or pressure for me to be anything other than what I was capable of in each moment. They held the fort for me while I took the time I needed to heal and see what was left of me in the end. A very few, close friends and workmates stood by me in this time and advocated and supported the choices that were best for me. I will be forever grateful and appreciative that I was blessed to have these people in my life.

As I healed, slowly and ever so unexpectedly, I remember a tiny piece of the puzzle of that one big job. A fragment that was real and not distorted by a thousand other jobs entwined in its memory. A breakthrough had happened. Now, over more days and weeks, the full events of that moment returned, and in the remembering, I was able to speak again. I started to add another and another sentence to the series of events that had happened that day and began to feel the emotions that were crushed into that sealed box. For each memory and emotion, it was an arduous and gruelling process to work through and bring resolution so they could no longer cause harm. Once I remembered this job, I could undertake to tackle the remaining flood of jobs held escaped from the now broken black box of my mind.

Learnings from this chapter...

1. You can survive more than you believe and you are stronger than you think. When you cannot cope with what lies ahead, just focus on getting through the next 30 seconds, and then the next 30 seconds and so on.
2. Even in the darkest moments there is still a star of light if we can only open our eyes and see it. You are never truly alone, if you dare to reach out for help.
3. Never ever give up.
4. When words won't come easily, use drawings or writing to get the thoughts out.

A DIFFERENT PERSON

"Remember that no matter what the problem, there is always a solution, and possibly many solutions. You just need to be willing to look for one and be willing to work and try it."
Shilpa Agarwal

Recovery from the PTSD was not an easy task and for every memory that was dealt with, another burst through. It now seemed that the triggers that prompted me to recall past jobs became more frequent and vast. Things that had been buried for 20 years would suddenly flash into my mind. Many were not distressing or difficult, but the ones that were each took time to work through and resolve.

When I eventually got to a point that I was well enough to return to work, I discovered that the paramedic that returned was a very different person to the one I had been before PTSD. In coming back to work with my colleagues I now just wanted to fit in and find some way to feel common ground with them. I started off working in the training room, teaching new students how to become Ambulance Officers, before progressing back into my on-road position in a graduated manner. This gave me the time to see if there were any residual effects from the PTSD that would make working impossible.

I have always been an optimist and a dreamer and have always been able to see the silver lining on even the darkest cloud. PTSD had taken me beyond that place and, at its worst, I was only able to see a tiny pinprick of light in the blackest blackness I had ever experienced. I was my own worst critique about whether I was capable of being a paramedic again, however through the gentle and expert care of my doctors, I was able to return to my position.

Back at work, I wanted to allow myself to be safe from the judgement and opinions of other, while sharing with my colleagues what this experience had been like. Some feared that my ability to cope with the job was diminished. I found that I was much more aware of the types of jobs I had never before attended, rather than how many I had seen before. My index of suspicion was higher when going to jobs where the information was not quite complete, and I had a much lower threshold of stress. The only benefit I felt in returning was I could again spend time with my colleagues who had experienced the same events.

I now found that work drained me and at the end of each shift I needed to be alone to restore the balance within me. More than ever now I craved my own company. My time away from work was spent not doing much, and my motivation levels were low. The intrinsic joy I felt about life had been taken from me and was now a forced entity. The best description I can give of this is like being myself, but cloaked and covered in an amour of grey. I felt numb, but anger and frustration came more easily.

More than all of that, I had now become acutely aware of the fragility of feeling secure about being a paramedic until my retirement. I often wondered whether this one big job I had seen was the worst that could happen and whether this episode of PTSD was to be my last. I had lost trust in the future and the ability to really know myself.

Through this seemingly emotionless time, I tried many things to find a new spark of interest. A steady stream of poor and expensive decisions ensued as I tried to fill the emptiness that PTDS had caused. I searched for new opportunities that might ignite the same passion within me that I experienced in the newness of my paramedic job.

I bought into courses which I thought may be interesting, then found that I didn't have the concentration to study. I bought material possessions to brighten my house and provide comfort, which I really couldn't afford. I borrowed money on a credit card and stopped taking notice of my finances. I signed up and paid to write this book and didn't have the courage to write the words at that time.

Life had become a cycle of work, get paid, spend money, work, get paid, spend money. As I lost control of my finances, the pressure grew. To fit in with my work peers, I bought a new car, because I could go away on 4WD weekends with them. With the new car, came the secret of disconnection I felt, caused by the shame of not being able to afford it.

My life had become dysfunctionally functional. To the outside world I had successfully overcome the PTSD and was thriving and prospering. Behind the scenes however, I felt like a sad failure of the person I had once been. My life was disorganised and flawed.

Although I recognised my inability to get organised and take control of my life again, my motivation was low. I struggled with conflicting feelings of wanting to be back at work and not having the passion for it any longer. Most of my time away from work was spent alone yet I craved company, especially that of my family. I had backed myself into a financial corner that meant I felt I had to stay in the job but I cared little about what I was spending. My connection to the world was predominantly from behind the safety of the screen of social media where I could post pictures and quotes of a happy life without the truth of it being seen.

One of the only things that helped me was exercise. I started to work one morning a week with an outdoor personal trainer. Being in nature brought a sense of calmto the chaos in my mind and I loved the feeling of being active. The joy of exercising in the outdoors led me to book a hike on one of the trails in New Zealand. Despite my inability to relate to the people I was trekking with, I renewed my deep sense of oneness to the bushlands, and this walk was the first inkling of knowing that I needed to reassess my life.

A few months later, a change of dynamics in the team at work highlighted for me the rut I had fallen into and prompted me to take notice of how my behaviour and attitudes were impacting my life. This self-reflection became another choice point in my life and I could finally see the possibility of how making different choices would open up more options. It was then I started to look for opportunities for what may come next.

At that time I had no idea if my direction would lead me down the path I was already on as a paramedic, or take me on an entirely new journey. What I did know right then was that if I stayed as a paramedic, I would need to change how I was working if I was to stay in the job until retirement. Either that, or I had to find my brave and make the choice to take a leap of faith and step onto a new path.

I guess you could liken how I was feeling to a piece of metal that has been melted in a furnace. It may have started off as an iron bar but is now a flattened bar. The shape has changed, but the essence is still the same. The metal can be heated again and remoulded into a beautiful sculpture and then polished until it shines.

Learnings from this chapter...

After the darkness of PTSD, change had occurred. Have you ever experienced an event that has changed who you have become? Here are a few of my favourite tips for dealing with the situation.

1. It is first important to acknowledge and validate what you feel before you can begin to challenge and change it.
2. It is when you recognise the changes that you can adapt to them and live in a new way.
3. Change takes courage and a willingness to admit that where you are in the moment is not a good place.
4. Always be open to change and explore all the options.

A NEW PATH

"You become the sum of the five people you spend the most time with. Surround yourself with positive people who champion your goals and dreams."
Stephanie Altus

Once I knew that change was needed and I started looking around and noticed the many and varied options that were available to me. My heart told me that it would take a drastic change to really know what I wanted but my head told me it needed to be a safe one. No burning bridges in this early phase.

Soon after I saw a job advertised looking for someone to go and work in the area where my daughter with the grandchildren lived. This was my chance, my safe alternate to what I was doing. I could go and be with my family for six months and stay working in the job I was already doing. There were no hard parts, I wouldn't have to sell my house and I could come home on my days off if I needed a break. I knew a couple of the staff at the new station and got on well with them, and I would return to my current workplace if it wasn't what I wanted after the secondment finished. I had previously done similar when I went to a new station and it had been a fantastic experience. So I took the position, packed up my car again with the few possessions I would need for a short stay, and headed off.

What happened next was to be the stepping stone to a whole new journey!

Living on the farm with my family was just the therapy I needed. The open spaces, fresh air, stunning views and scenery gave me the link back to nature that I craved. Coming home from work to my daughter and grandchildren was a huge and positive distraction at the end of each work day. It gave me a chance to talk when I needed it. Helping with the chores made me feel useful, and needed in a way that mattered. And helping with the animals gave me many moments of laughter at their antics.

At work I was exposed to working with new people, different types of jobs, alternate ways of doing things and new conversations. Learning my way around this new area was made all the more fun by a workmate who taught me the history of where I was now residing. He often took me off the usual route when driving back to station from jobs to show me interesting places and points of interest.

One of my favourite people to work with was a girl who inspired me on every single shift, with her tenacity and bubbly attitude to life. In her, I remembered who I had been before I got lost in PTSD. I settled in quickly, got on well with my peers and loved every single day of my time there.

One of the best aspects of the job up there was meeting patients who had already celebrated their 100th birthday.

In conversations with them I learned more about life that I had ever before pondered. These patients gave me a new zest for my own life and I began to have a future focus rather than being stuck in the past.

Not long before I was to return to my usual position, I attended the first road fatality I had ever been to in my career. Immediately upon reading the job screen and seeing what we were going to, I was filled with trepidation and an expectation of the carnage we would see. On arrival the reality was even worse than I had conjured up in my mind before we got there. As always, I stepped into a mode of automaticity and did all the things I knew to do and had been taught in my learning.

Once the patients had all been treated and transported off to hospitals, I stood on the edge of this scene and all the familiar feelings of over thinking started to happen. Again I knew I was at a choice point in life; I could let these feelings overwhelm me and end up succumbing to the darkness of PTSD again or I could immediately ask for help in that moment and see what I was left with after a debrief. I chose to ask!

It was after this case that I came to understand that how and what I felt after these jobs was actually a reflection of what many paramedics feel in the same situations. Up till now I had just not been courageous enough to speak up and ask for help early on. This job taught me acceptance of who I was, and that it is okay to have a big heart that hurts in the face of absolute tragedy. It was then I knew it is ok to see the hurt and pain of others and feel deep empathy without their pain becoming your pain. And I knew I could still do the job I needed to do in the moment, and deal with my own feelings once it was completed. I learned to trust myself again and found self-forgiveness.

Not only did this change help me to grow, but it challenged me as well. Many of you will know that when we decide to change our living arrangements it can be a stressful time. I had gone from living in my big home all alone, to being in a house filled with my family. I no longer had all my familiar things around me or the quietness and dysfunctional routines I had set up for myself in my own home. Suddenly, here I was, thrown into all the mayhem and enjoyment of a home filled with children.

Instead of coming home to an empty house, I was coming home to the welcoming squeals and hugs of my grandchildren. I was coming home to the intelligent and philosophical discussions with my teen granddaughter and daughter. I was coming home to laughter, fun and a most welcome cup of tea awaiting me on the bench. The simple pleasures of life were there every time I stepped through the door.

I often found myself contemplating life while watching the antics of these children. Little kids are so real about life, they live it as they experience it with no question of whether it is good or bad, right or wrong. When they are little they do not have wants, only needs, and once these needs are met, they are happy again. They are curious and fascinated by life and are in a constant flow of learning as they experience their world. And when they have had enough they seek comfort and take time to rest and recuperate before it begins again in each new day.

In my teen granddaughter, I saw her raised awareness of who she was and the questioning of who she was becoming as she moved further and further into her experience of the world. I was in awe of her ability to discuss her version of life as she saw it and I loved these conversations with her. She taught me about life from the eyes of the young and instilled back in me a fresh new perspective.

And I loved watching my daughter be a mother to her own children. I was proud of her ability to balance love and the challenges of parenting, despite being a busy working mother. To see her achieve such a variety of objectives and still make time to chat and connect was amazing, and to know that she had opened her home to welcome me for this time was a true gift.

Being outside more was another huge benefit of this new adventure and being on the farm meant there were many reasons to get out and breathe in the fresh air. It brought back memories of my childhood days of growing up in the freedom of the bush, when I loved to wander in nature, I loved the expanse of the paddocks to amble freely and in these outdoor moments, it occurred to me that I had gotten into a pattern in my own home of not opening up my curtains; I had been leaving them closed to keep the world out. I made a decision then and there that once I returned home, each day I would throw open my curtains and welcome the morning.

One of the things that increased in my awareness was my own need to find a balance between alone time and being with people. In a job where we are constantly giving and caring, it can drain us, both physically and mentally. We need to make the time to be in our own space and recoup our energy.

This time away allowed me to spend more time with my younger daughter as well, and to have many beautiful shared moments. Spending time with her was (and has always been) my "cool mum" time. She takes me on outings where I get to experience places and things that I would never have thought of trying on my own. Living in the city, she knew all the "in" places to do fun stuff. I loved that she gifted to me these fun moments of time with her and that we could laugh and talk together with the freedom of trust and love. Her home in my time away also became a quiet break from noise of the farm without having to be alone. Alone in bed, lying in the dark quietness of night at her house, I had time to think about the immense gratitude I feel in having my children and grand children, and the pride and joy they bring to my life.

Throughout everything I had been through and all that was occurring now, I looked at my family and in them I saw inspiration. In the babies I saw acceptance and being in the moment, in my teen granddaughter and daughters I saw courage and all the achievements they were making. Their unwavering ability to face each problem, find a solution and move forward helped me to find my own peace and start to find a way towards the future. And in all of them I found love and connection and a reflection of myself. I knew in my heart I had been a part of who they were, and I owed it to them to show courage and become my best self again.

Having the benefit of this time away from what had become my normal was starting to bring about the emergence, the new me. This was a time of reconnecting with the inner little girl who had been so fearless and free in my childhood, and with the woman who had set big goals despite the odds and had fervently achieved them.

More and more, I started to see a clear picture of who I wanted to be again and the vision of how I wanted my future to look was slowly growing. As I reflected on the events that had brought me here, it was crystal clear that I had the choice and power to create whatever future I chose. My feisty will to create a new future had developed and my smile and laughter had returned.

What I was certain of by the time I left this place was that, for me, this job was now becoming harder. Every new case I attended piled up in my mind on top of the previous ones I held in my memory. The time had come to be open to start looking for what else I could do and a whole new direction. It was on the farm that I really appreciated the importance of the balance between work and my personal life. I acknowledged to, myself that family was still my most important value.

New choices and directions were already developing in my mind. Life is for learning and growing in who we are, and as we begin to know more about ourselves we expand our awareness and gain the courage to take the next step. I had now returned to all that was important to me. Perhaps, in the burning ashes of tragedy, the phoenix of who I was at my core had returned and I had tapped back into my soul space.

Learnings from this chapter...

1. When you are not sure, say yes and see where it takes you.
2. It is said that you don't know what you don't know until you know it. Always keep your mind open to learning. Look for the lessons and allow yourself to grow and expand with each new experience.
3. If you want new results you need to do something different. You will not make changes by doing what you have always done.

———— CHAPTER 12 ————

A NEW DREAM

"There comes a moment in life where you want more and it is time to take the next step. Very few people grab this moment and never look back."
Stephanie Altus

Have you ever dared to dream? Did you follow this dream and steadfastly take action to make it a reality? Or did you falter and cover it with a veil of being too fearful to try?

Then came the day that it was time to go home! It was time to take all the things I had discovered during this sojourn and use them to design the next chapters of my life. These chapters were the ones I wanted to be filled with stories of new paths and new roads travelled; of exploring and of the joy of finding all the treasures there are still to be found in the world.

I knew if I was to change my future; I first had to take a stock of exactly where I was at, dream a little to decide where I wanted to be, make a plan to achieve it, and then start to take action steps to make it happen. It was now I thought back a little in time to the strategies that had helped me in the past. I got out my gratitude journal and diligently filled it in day by day, and my bucket list that had been pushed aside for too long. Over the next month I took loads of self-time to take stock of where I was currently at in my life. I did an audit and looked at the courses I had enrolled in, my finances, my routines, my home filled with possessions, my job, what I was passionate about and my thoughts and beliefs. I took the time to ponder how each of these made me feel.

Once I had done the audit, I identified what I needed to keep and what I could discard. I took my bucket list and chose just **1 Big Goal** that I was going to focus on and tick off before another year had passed me by. I wanted a goal that would challenge me enough to scare me but was doable with enough effort and within 12 months. It had to be multifaceted to allow me to stretch my boundaries and grow in multiple areas of my life. Along the way to achieving it, I wanted to be able to learn new skills and tick off some of my smaller bucket list items. Most of all it had to have a positive impact on my mind, as well as my body and mind, as well as making a positive difference for others.

If I was truly serious about changing my life and making the rest of it my best time ever, I had to value myself first. First I needed to challenge my limiting beliefs and create new ones that would support this new path I was about to take. I had to develop and apply new ways of being and doing things in my life. I had to take more time for myself and use it effectively to become all of who I wanted to become.

I had met a couple of bubbly bright women who seemed to be living life in the way I craved, and decided to follow their mentorship to create my own dare to dream life. I took a risk on myself and went back to the lady I had chosen to help me in writing my book and I reset my contract with her to publish my story. I got myself a life coach who challenged my thinking and guided me as I created a more productive and positive mindset. I enrolled in a new course that would support me in completing the other courses I had previously taken on. I dragged out all of the things I had started over the last few years, kept the ones that would fit into this new path I was creating and discarded the rest.

This life audit showed me that I had been stuck in a rut in my thinking with the PTSD for too long, and my passion for my job and life had started to fade. I was unhealthy, unfit, overweight, over 50, and financially broke. I had wasted too much time on procrastination, and was disconnected from the people who mattered most to me and to my community. My home had become cluttered and disorganised and I had been stagnant for too long.

The job of a paramedic is by necessity an extroverted role. You need to be able to be out in the community, taking control, making rapid decisions and communicating across a wide range of situations. In my role, I am able to wear this hat and become this personality and give my best on each shift I work. But by nature I am an introvert and time alone is a must for me to recharge, restore and replenish the energy my job saps from me. Identifying this within myself helped me to make my decision on what to do next.

In that instant I closed my eyes, forgave my failings and decided on my **1 Big Goal**. In one year from now, I was going to walk EL CAMINO! Then I sighed a long drawn out breath of relief and knew with conviction and certainty that my life was about to change dramatically. A smile slowly spread across my face and my eyes brightened at the thought of achieving this long held dream. It held all the criteria I needed to improve every aspect of my life and I would be ticking off a number of other bucket list items on the journey to achieving this one.

Two days later it was booked.

I now had the focus and direction I needed to start taking action, and began to take those small steps that are needed once we make a decision to begin a new journey.

Learnings from this chapter...

Are you ready to begin a new chapter in your life? Do you have a dream that you have had for too long? Is it time you turned the dream into a goal and started to take action to achieve it?

1. Trust yourself. So far you have survived 100% of what life has thrown at you.
2. Take an audit of your life and be open to an honest appraisal of where you are currently at with your life.
3. Take the time to ponder what may be, explore it, then be brave enough to go out and get it.
4. Never be afraid to leave behind what does not work for you any longer.
5. Surround yourself with positive role models who will help you achieve your goals.

COUCH TO CAMINO

The most poignant event that changed everything for me was a very tiny moment on the Christmas day after I had returned home from my secondment. My daughters gave me a beautiful family photo of themselves and all my grandchildren with Santa. A family picture that was as beautiful as it was sad for me, and tears welled up in my eyes–I was the only one absent. My promise to myself was to create a life where I would never again have to miss out on these precious times with my family.

I committed to myself that whatever I did into the future would be with a focus to include and involve them. My legacy will be to create a life that they can share with me and to show them that living life on your own terms is your birthright. Somehow, as I returned to my usual position at work, I would find a way to get back to creating more time for my family and finding my full passion for life.

My greatest learnings from all I have been through is, that to absolutely be centered in our lives we must always go back to our heart space, find what fires our passion and live our lives true to our values and our soul space.

By nature I am a free spirit and a wild child who loves nothing more than to be in nature. To have the freedom to wander at will and dance to the music I have in my heart. My children and grandchildren are the lifeblood that empower me to be my best and will always be my greatest love. I am an introvert and make friends slowly but my loyalty runs deep. I care too much and I will always have a heart as big as eternity. My life will never be shades of grey, it will always be filled with a whole spectrum of colour and sparkle. I make no apology for any of this, I am who I am.

So as I start working towards this **1 Big Goal** to walk the Camino, let me share with you a little of what it actually is and what steps I will be taking before I start walking this trail in 12 months' time.

The Camino I will be walking is a pilgrim trek of nearly 800 km across Northern Spain. It starts at St Jean Pied de Port in the French Alps on the border of Spain and stretches to finish at the Cathedral of Santiago de Compostela. It is a spiritual path that leads to the burial site of the apostle St James, who it is thought to be buried in Santiago.

The trail is walked by thousands of pilgrims every year for as many and more reasons. Most travel by foot but some also by bike, horseback or donkey. For most who choose to walk this path, it is seen as a spiritual adventure in which they can take a break from the bustle of modern life and return to the simplicity of nature and connection with themselves and others.

For this goal to become a reality I have set myself mini goals to reach in stages until I leave for my trip. These mini goals are focussed around my mindset, finances, fitness, decluttering my posessions and getting my life organised, creating routines and the completion of writing this book. Each day I do something more that takes me another step closer to creating the life I choose, by the success that comes from completing the mini goals I have set.

Is it hard work? Yes! Are some of the tasks challenging? Yes! Is it fun? Yes!

Is it worth it? A resounding yes!

In writing this book, I get to share it with a wonderful mentor and we have had a ball bringing it to life. As I improve my fitness, I get to share it with a wonderful personal trainer who inspires me with her fitness and zest for life. I also share my walks with my family and friends, to some of the most beautiful nature areas in our state.

The most brilliant thing to come out of following my heart towards this big goal has been the choice and opportunity to build a business around my own journey and in turn, I will help others to achieve their dreams. This fires my passion! I am absolutely loving this new work I am doing, and every day I get to work towards another goal that excites me.

I still work as a paramedic for now and my passion for this job has been reignited by finding a balance between the work that is so familiar and I have loved for so long, alongside the challenge ahead to achieve my 1 Big Goal. In the process I am returning to the optimism and hope that sits inside my soul and I have a deep peace that wherever I wander next in my life, is exactly where I should be. When I am at work I serve those who need me in that role 100% and in my time off I now give 100% to living my ideal life.

As I take the actions in preparation for my Camino walk, I reflect on my bucket list and how this came about. So many of us have wishes and even bucket lists. Like me, many have dumped these into a drawer or cupboard, hidden from sight. But what is the point of having dreams if they are discarded and forgotten?

Having a bucket list can sometimes be an overwhelming reminder of all the things you are missing out on in life, but it can also be a prompt for all the things we would love to do if time and money were no object to us. Pick just one thing and make it your **1 Big Goal**. Put a timeframe on it, and take the action steps to make it happen.

If you are not sure if you can achieve it and need some coaching to help you along like I did, contact me through my Facebook page **1 Big Goal**.

My bucket list is no longer hidden away in the depths of a drawer, but now takes pride of a place on a clip on my office wall. When I return from my walk and I have successfully completed my Camino, I will proudly tick it off and decide which item will be my next 1 Big Goal.

Learnings from this chapter...

Do you have a dare-to-dream list of things you would love to do? Here's how to make it happen:

1. Pick one goal to start with and create a clear vision of what it looks like.
2. Write down all the steps you need to take to achieve it and start by taking one small step each day towards it.
3. Share your goal with others and enjoy sharing the path you walk to make it happen.
4. Life is not about the destination, it is about having fun and enjoying the journey.
5. Dare to do what you dream and life will always be an adventure.
6. When you find what you love, do it and you will never work a day in your life.

If you are at a choice point in life and unsure of which direction to go, contact me. As an inspirational coach - I'm the person who's done this, I'm the person who's set many big goals and achieved them. I'm the person who's done it by taking the little steps over and over again, and then more steps until I got to that place of success and achievement. I'm also the person who's fallen along the way, so I can resonate with that. I can understand that happens when you set yourself big goals and the effort and reward that comes from moving towards it. At the end when you achieve your own goal, I will be there cheering you along and celebrating your success. I can walk beside you to hold you accountable until your dare-to-dream has become a reality.

Thank You Note

In writing this book, I have had a long journey to reach this place where it is finally published. My story is ready to be shared with others in the hope that they may find comfort and inspiration in its pages. May the readers know that they are never alone and support is all around them, if they only find the courage to ask and to know that being stuck in a dark place does not have to be the end of their story. They have the ability to choose a new path, set themselves their own 1 Big Goal and move towards a future that can be extraordinary.

Along my road I have had the good fortune of having many people who have supported me and have walked beside me for every step, those who have joined the journey for a short distance, those who have been my guides and those who helped me to take the next step when I could no longer walk alone, and those who trusted me enough that when I needed to rest would allow it, trustingthat I had it within myself to get back up and follow my own path again.

My two beautiful daughters and my grand-daughter have been my constant companions on this avenue of life. I thank them for allowing me my failings, cheering on my successes, tolerating my hairy ideas and supporting me every step of the way. They make me laugh and inspire me to go out and follow my dreams, no matter how impossible they may seem. There have been moments of tears and frustration in the battle through PTSD, but never once did they turn their backs or leave me to fight alone. To them I am forever grateful and I love them with all of my soul.

To my Grandpa, who is no longer living on this earth, but now lives in my heart and as a part of who I am, in all the cells of my being. I thank him for giving me courage to be myself. For always trusting and encouraging me to lead my own journey, and gave me the confidence to know that I could succeed in anything I truely wanted. I love him for being my constant in a world of uncertainty.

There are so many people who have shared my life and this journey;

To my beautiful friends – you each give to me a little sunshine in my days and loads of fun and laughter.

Diann, through getting to know you and sharing our stories, I have come to know myself better. I have loved all the little things I have ticked off my bucket list through the Gummies group, and in Fiji, I learnt to just relax, be still and allow time to decide my own path. .

To my work colleagues who have supported me and shared in this horrible diagnosis that is PTSD, and have then supported me more to keep doing the work I love – I thank you from the bottom of my heart. Without you there were many times where I may not have been able to continue, but your words of encouragement got me back up and helped me to become the best paramedic I could be. You know who you all are and I truly understand the concept of camaraderie.

To Phil, you saw the most broken paramedic and stepped in to protect and guide me back from that darkest place. You never waivered in your trust that I could fight this beast and always knew under your gentle direction that I would find my way back. My thanks and gratitude will always remain for you.

To my medical physicians and specialists, I thank you for your dedication to your professions and for providing expert care with kindness, when I most needed it. I am so grateful for the hours you spent listening to my pain and helping me heal, until it finally got to a level I can now manage.

To Tom, thank you for coaching me when I was ready to take those first tentative steps out of the darkness. Your guidance and trust in me was absolutely life changing and I could not have asked for a more gentle but effective mentor to teach me to find myself and to walk again.

Shilpa and Akhilesh, without you both this book would not exist. Your patience in waiting till I could get the words out and the new methods you created to make sure I was safe to speak were an absolute blessing. Thank you for helping me bring my book to life. Also to the book editors, cover designers, publishing crew and all other involved in bringing my book from thoughts through to a real book I can hold and share.

Jodie and Amy, you girls are an absolute inspiration. Once I was emerging out of the darkness, you opened my eyes to a world of possibility. From my small ideas, you helped me to define the path forward and have been encouraging me to take the new and exciting paths that I feared at the start. I look forward to working with you into the future to grow this journey.

To everyone who has been part of my life up until now and part of all the stages I have been through, thank you for being a part of this incredible journey.

Each person enters our lives for a reason – to teach us something or to learn from us or maybe both. If I have not mentioned anyone in this list, please know you have not been forgotten. Through all the ups and downs of life many people have come and gone, many have left me with lessons that will serve me well into the future, and many remain as the friends I choose to take forward. My life has been absolutely blessed with so much wonderful and as I follow my 1 Big Goal to walk the Camino, I am excited for a future filled with a whole world of new people to meet and new experiences.

References

Black Dog Institute
https://www.blackdoginstitute.org.au/

Beyondblue
1300 22 4636
https://www.beyondblue.org.au/

Lifeline
Crisis helpline 13 11 14
https://www.lifeline.org.au/

1Big Goal
https://www.facebook.com/1BigGoal/

Cartwright Coaching
https://www.facebook.com/tomcartwrightcoaching/

The 7 Effect
https://www.facebook.com/the7effect/

Want Solution
https://www.facebook.com/wantsolution/

www.ingramcontent.com/pod-product-compliance
Lightning Source LLC
Chambersburg PA
CBHW051456130726
47987CB00005B/2335